American Social Welfare Policy

REASSESSMENT AND REFORM

American Social Welfare Policy

REASSESSMENT AND REFORM

MARC L. MIRINGOFF

Fordham University School of Social Service

SANDRA OPDYCKE

Hudson River Psychiatric Center

PRENTICE-HALL
Englewood Cliffs, New Jersey 07632

Library of Congress Cataloging-in-Publication Data

Miringoff, Marc L.
  American social welfare policy.

  Includes bibliographies and index.
  1. United States—Social policy. 2. Public welfare—
United States. I. Opdycke, Sandra. II. Title.
HV95.M57 1986   361.6′1′0973   85-23837
ISBN 0-13-029554-X

Cover design: George Cornell
Manufacturing buyer: John B. Hall

Printed in the United States of America

10 9 8 7 6 5 4 3 2 1

ISBN 0-13-029554-X   01

Prentice-Hall International (UK) Limited, *London*
Prentice-Hall of Australia Pty. Limited, *Sydney*
Prentice-Hall Canada Inc., *Toronto*
Prentice-Hall Hispanoamericana, S.A., *Mexico*
Prentice-Hall of India Private Limited, *New Delhi*
Prentice-Hall of Japan, Inc., *Tokyo*
Prentice-Hall of Southeast Asia Pte. Ltd., *Singapore*
Editora Prentice-Hall do Brasil, Ltda., *Rio de Janeiro*
Whitehall Books Limited, *Wellington, New Zealand*

For Helen S. Miringoff,
whose life taught us concern and compassion
and the ways in which they are sustained

For Dorothy and Datus Smith,
who have always looked where the land is bright,
and have helped to make it brighter

Contents

Foreword

By the spring of 1983, I had thought about and worked on this book for several years. The agreement with Prentice-Hall had been reached, the book's theoretical framework and themes were developed, the first four chapters were written, the rest was outlined. At that point I was offered the position of assistant dean of the Fordham University School of Social Service with administrative responsibility for its campus in Tarrytown, N.Y. As the tasks of my new position became apparent, it was clear that I needed assistance in completing the book. I turned to a colleague, Sandra Opdycke. Sandra and I had worked together at the community level, where the results of policy are most felt. She was director of Quality Assurance of the Hudson River Psychiatric Center, a state hospital of the New York State Department of Mental Health. She is now the hospital's associate director. Sandra and I have worked together for nearly a year and a half completing the manuscript. Her contribution has been essential. It is now our book.

Marc Miringoff

Authors' Note

This book is intended primarily for use in social policy courses at the graduate level. Although it does discuss the basic services of the social welfare institution and their historical development, its purpose is to raise questions about social welfare and to suggest directions for positive change. As such, *American Social Welfare Policy: Reassessment and Reform* is best used as a complement to a work that contains a comprehensive presentation of the programs and policies of social welfare. It is our hope that, used in this way, the book will help to increase students' ability to analyze and understand social welfare and to broaden their awareness about its functioning and its future.

Preface

In the past fifteen to twenty years our society has come to recognize a host of social problems. More than ever before, issues like drug abuse, child abuse, mental illness, alcoholism, and family breakdown have emerged as issues of critical national concern. At the same time, specific groups in society, such as blacks, Hispanics, women, the aging, and the disabled, have intensified their efforts to ensure that their particular problems win a place on the public agenda. Combined with the perennial concerns of income maintenance, housing, health care, and employment, these recent developments have added a new intensity to America's recognition of its social problems.

Yet, during the same period, another phenomenon has occurred: a growing antipathy toward public social welfare as an American institution. In both the liberal and conservative communities there is apparent agreement that the welfare state—the planned active participation of government in the alleviation of social problems—has for the most part failed. Several factors have contributed to this development. One is the traditional, almost instinctive ambivalence about government in American society. "Society in every state is a blessing, but Government, even in its best state, is but a necessary evil," wrote Thomas Paine. This viewpoint has been an important element in the American value system throughout our history.

Until recently, the public's view of government had been relatively positive. The remarkable initiatives of the New Deal era, the winning of World War II, the prosperity of the 1950s, and the popularity of presidents such as Franklin Roosevelt, Dwight Eisenhower, and John Kennedy all helped to allay Americans' doubts about government's role. But the events of the late 1960s began a dramatic shift in attitude. The tragedy and bitterness of the Vietnam war was the first blow. Hawk and dove seemed to agree on one thing only: in matters of life and death, the government could not control events. Other blows followed: urban unrest, Watergate, national economic problems, the hostages in Iran. Increasingly, government came to be seen as ineffective and intrusive rather than as a source of mutual strength and support.

This growing distrust of government has influenced Americans' perception of social welfare. "Big government," "big business," and "big" programs have become easy targets, and the political parade that has marched against them has been varied and impressive. The contenders in every presidential campaign since 1968 have worn the antigovernment mantle. Nixon assumed it in 1968; Nixon, Wallace, and to some extent McGovern in 1972; Ford, Carter, and Wallace in 1976; both Carter and Reagan in 1980; and Reagan and even Mondale in 1984. Countless candidates in local elections have joined the chorus.

Social welfare programs themselves have provided ammunition for government's critics. Some public programs have been perceived as inefficient and unsuccessful. Others have been viewed as intrusive; in these cases, public doubts have been sharpened with a backlash of resentment. This reaction has been particularly forceful concerning such highly publicized and controversial programs as busing, affirmative action, and the large-scale release of mental patients to the community. Again and again, it has seemed, in social welfare as in other areas, that government has made unrealistic promises and then failed to deliver on them.

The current crisis facing American social welfare, then, is paradoxical, for at a time when effective social intervention seems most essential, it is also seen as least desirable. This poses an important question: Is there something about the way in which social welfare has been conceived and implemented that is preventing its acceptance as an American institution? And, if this is the case, are there different policy directions and program concepts that would add strength to social welfare? In addressing these questions, many fundamental issues arise. What values are implicit in our policies and programs? To what extent do they reflect the general values of society, and how are they at odds? Is human service expertise used in a manner that assures the highest level of program effectiveness? Is the current organizational structure of social welfare the best one possible in the context of the resources currently available? And, finally, how can a better understanding of these issues help to increase the benefits of social welfare to society and thereby gain increased public support?

This book will examine these issues. In preparing our analysis, we make no claim to neutrality. We believe that social welfare and its human services are good and necessary activities for our society, but we accept the premise that they are in fact in danger and that reassessment and reform have come to be essential tasks. Such an endeavor is not always pleasant. It must involve the admission of past error, the recognition that approaches have been tried without sufficient consideration and promises proclaimed without developing the mechanisms by which they could be realized. It is, however, our hope that this book will be sufficiently informative and evocative to increase both the scope and quality of debate about the future of social welfare in American society, a debate that can serve as a prelude to constructive action.

American Social Welfare Policy

REASSESSMENT AND REFORM

CHAPTER ONE

American Social Welfare: The Policy Pendulum

There have been periods in American history in which the nation's leaders have moved decisively to embrace social welfare as an issue of public concern and responsibility. Woodrow Wilson, in his first Inaugural Address, for instance, placed special emphasis on

> . . . the means by which government may be put at the service of humanity, in safeguarding the health of the Nation, the health of its men and its women and its children as well as their rights in the struggle for existence. . . . There can be no equality or opportunity, the first essential of justice in the body politic, if men and women and children be not shielded in their lives, their very vitality, from the consequences of great industrial and social processes which they can not alter, control, or singly cope with.[1]

Two decades later, Franklin Roosevelt echoed this view, emphasizing the obligation of society in general, and government in particular, to enhance individuals' welfare:

> Among our objectives I place the security of the men, women and children of the Nation first. . . . Security was attained in earlier days through the interdependence of members of families upon each other and of the families within a small community upon each other. The complexities of great communities and of organized industry make less real these simple means of security. Therefore, we are compelled to employ the active interest of the Nation as a whole through government in order to encourage a greater security for each individual who composes it.[2]

At other times, political leaders have explicitly disavowed a public role in social welfare, stressing instead the importance of self-determination. Herbert Hoover's speech on "The Philosophy of Rugged Individualism" in 1928 expressed this view, contrasting the governmental activism that had been necessary during World War I with the more decentralized policies of the 1920s.

> We were challenged with a peace-time choice between the American system of rugged individualism and a European philosophy of diametrically opposed doctrines—doctrines of paternalism and state socialism. The acceptance of these ideas would have meant the destruction of self-government through centralization of government. It would have meant the undermining of the individual initiative and enterprise through which our people have grown to unparalleled greatness. . . . When the Republican Party came into full power it went at once resolutely back to our fundamental conception of the state and the rights and responsibilities of the individual.[3]

The same viewpoint was expressed by President Eisenhower in 1957.

> All of us can sense a disturbing disposition on the part of many groups throughout our land to seek solutions to their problems from sources outside themselves.

Because life today is more complex and interdependent than ever before, we seem, in every difficulty always more ready to lean on government than upon ourselves. Such an approach to our individual and group problems can never retain the health and vigor of America. Rather, we must believe in and practice an approach founded on individual initiative, individual self-reliance and resourcefulness, individual conscience, and individual voluntary effort.[4]

Public policy on social welfare can, in fact, be viewed as a pendulum, moving between times of expansion and contraction, between initiative and consolidation. In this century there have been three notable periods of expansion and initiative in social welfare, each followed by a period in which the pendulum has swung back toward contraction and consolidation. The Progressive Era, the period from the turn of the century to the First World War, was one period of expansion, a time of great advance for social welfare at the local and state levels. The New Deal of the 1930s represented the next period of growth, perhaps the single most important era in American history in terms of social welfare legislation and initiative. The third period of expansion, particularly in the areas of poverty, job training, medical care, and civil rights, came in the 1960s, with the programs of the New Frontier and Great Society.

In between these periods, the pendulum swung back. The Harding, Coolidge, and Hoover administrations of the 1920s, the Truman and Eisenhower years of the 1940s and 1950s, and the Nixon, Carter, Ford, and Reagan years of the 1970s and 1980s were all predominantly periods of contraction, reassessment, and consolidation, with few new initiatives or legislation in the area of social welfare.

Each of the three periods of expansion—the Progressive Era, the 1930s, and the 1960s—produced new programs and benefits for people suffering from social problems. Each period represented a temporary consensus, an agreement that concerted action was necessary, that social conditions demanded public response. At this end of the pendulum's swing, decisions were made, legislation passed, and new programs conceived and implemented. But the swing of the pendulum involves more than a sudden decision to pass social legislation. Forces both inside and outside government must work in complementary ways to bring about a period of expansion in social welfare.

THE INSIDE AND OUTSIDE PROCESSES

Frequently, it is the process outside government that comes first. Advocacy organizations, recipient groups, charismatic individuals, scholars, and journalists contribute to the ferment, identifying issues, calling for change, offering specific ideas and proposals for solving the problems they have identified. Writing, speaking, agitating, educating, these groups play a critical role in making the general public aware of the issues at stake. "Again and again," writes Barbara Ward, "it is through the small catalyzing group, fighting for a particular issue . . . that political action suddenly comes alive and the indifferent ward or apathetic commune begins to hum like a hive of bees."[5] At a period ripe for social change, a great number of such groups often flourish simultaneously, offering different solutions and different approaches, yet serving together to arouse public interest and concern.[6]

Clearly, the contributions of the outside process are highly important to the expansion of social welfare. But they cannot begin to achieve their goals until there is a complementary inside process, a group of responsive individuals inside government with whom to work. Public agitation may force unsympathetic officeholders to grant a few legislative points as a way of making peace, but significant social change requires a more synergistic political environment. The three principal periods of expansion we have mentioned—the Progressive Era, the 1930s, and the 1960s—all took place when there existed within government a group of political leaders who had a real commitment to furthering social change. Sensitive to the arguments of the outside process, yet often more attuned than the outsiders to the political realities of policymaking, these officeholders were the ones who actually initiated the changes sought. It was their task—through a combination of argument, compromise, debate, public relations, and diplomacy—to bring to reality the expansion of social welfare that those outside government originally worked for.

We have discussed the inside and outside processes as if the latter always preceded the former and as if the inside and outside processes always involved different actors. Neither is necessarily true. Some reforms are initiated inside government, with those outside only responding after the fact. Sometimes leaders of the outside process take roles inside government, and sometimes the reverse occurs. Sometimes ideas for social change take so long to find their way into the policymaking process that it is difficult to analyze precisely what roles the inside and outside processes played in their emergence. What seems clear is that the movement of the pendulum toward the expansion of social welfare requires the energies and contributions of both those in office and those in the broader community.

To illustrate this interaction, let us examine the three periods of significant social welfare expansion and note in each case the processes inside and outside government that were involved in their development.[7]

The Progressive Era (1900–1917)

The Progressive Era marked a major shift in American history, moving the perception of social welfare from "charity" to "social policy." During this period, social problems gradually came to be viewed in institutional as well as individual terms.[8] Organizations outside government, like the Charity Organization Society (COS), underwent this transformation early, and helped influence similar changes nationwide. The COS was begun in 1877 as an effort to stimulate the moral regeneration of the poor on a case-by-case basis. Soon after 1900, however, it began to focus more heavily on initiating social change.[9] The COS Pittsburgh Survey, for example, was an important contribution in this direction, being one of the first systematic examinations of poverty and social problems. Because it focused on the large-scale needs of an urban population rather than on the deficiencies of poor individuals, it helped advance social legislation in the years that followed.[10] Cox and Garvin note that "out of the Pittsburgh Survey came a council of social agencies which took upon itself the responsibility for acting upon the recommendations of the survey and conducting additional studies and reforms."[11] The survey was replicated in many other cities, providing the basis for state and municipal social reform across the nation.[12]

The settlement house movement was another important spearhead to the advancement of social welfare during the Progressive Era. The first settlement house in America was opened in 1886, but the great proliferation occurred in the decade after 1900. By 1910 more than 400 settlement houses had been established.[13] They were initiated as residential and community-oriented centers outside government, but under the leadership of such socially oriented settlement workers as Jane Addams and Florence Kelley, they quickly began to define social problems in legislative terms. Soon the settlement workers were pressing for governmental reforms in the areas of child labor, child welfare, factory safety, juvenile courts, court reform, women's suffrage, public health, and social insurance programs such as workmen's compensation, old-age pensions, aid to the blind, and mothers' aid.[14]

The settlement house workers directed their efforts to both state and federal levels of government. At the state level, they influenced officeholders to pass child labor laws, establish juvenile court systems, and initiate America's first social insurance programs.[15] At the federal level, they induced President Theodore Roosevelt to hold a White House Conference on Child Welfare in 1909, which led to the establishment of the federal Children's Bureau in 1912.[16] The settlement workers' most ambitious effort at the federal level was their participation in developing the Keating-Owen Bill, which prohibited child labor. The law was passed by the Congress in 1916 but declared unconstitutional in 1918. It was nevertheless significant in setting a precedent for child labor legislation later enacted during the New Deal.[17]

The settlement house workers multiplied the influence of what we have termed the outside process through community organization networks. Associations affiliated with the settlement house programs included the Women's Trade Union League, the National Child Labor Committee, the National Consumers League, and the General (National) Federation of Women's Clubs.[18] Through this organizational work the settlement house movement encouraged the National Conference on Charities and Corrections to cooperate in legislative activities on behalf of children and families.[19] The settlement house workers also helped minority groups to develop organizational affiliations, adding new voices to the outside process. The National Association for the Advancement of Colored People (NAACP) was organized in 1909 with the support of Jane Addams, Florence Kelley, and Lillian Wald—all leaders of the settlement house movement. The Urban League and the Immigrant Protective League were also developed with coalitional support.[20]

The settlement house workers were of course only one element in a nationwide reform movement that involved a wide range of groups and individuals inside and outside government. Contributing to the outside process was a lively combination of writers, teachers, clergymen, social workers, neighborhood and ethnic leaders, workers' groups, and interested citizens. More and more through these years, the issue of public responsibility for individual welfare was brought to public attention.

But the advocacy engendered by the outside process, however passionate, could not alone have moved the policy pendulum of social welfare. Increasingly during the Progressive Era, social reform was pursued by those inside government as well as those outside. Sometimes outsiders moved into elected positions, and sometimes established politicians became more sympathetic to reform. Gradually the inside process became an important element in the development of social welfare. Mayors like Tom Johnson of Cleveland, and governors like John Altgeld of Illinois were joined by hundreds of other officeholders at every level of state and local government sympathetic to reform. Even more radical reformers gained public support; by 1912, 1,000 Socialists held office in 33 states and 160 cities.[21] Building on the principle that government could be cost-effective as well as humane, that reform could serve self-interest as well as altruism, this new generation of political leadership provided vivid demonstrations of how community energies could be pooled to address social problems. Concerns for social justice and reform were stressed, not in the context of class-specific charity, but rather as one facet of activist good government, intervening at multiple levels to improve the quality of life for all citizens.

The efforts of reformers inside and outside government received their greatest recognition at the national level in 1912, when their demands for social policy legislation were incorporated into the Progressive Party platform. Included were planks on child welfare, adult and child labor, and social insurance. Jane Addams, who seconded Theodore Roosevelt's nomination, said of this program: ''The Progressive platform contains all the things I have been fighting for for more than a decade.''[22] Yet, even though the Progressive Party lost strength steadily after 1912, the movement that gave it birth left a remarkable history of reform at the state and local levels, a tribute to the complementary efforts of those inside and outside government during the Progressive Era.

1918–1933: The Pendulum Swings Back

During the 1920s social welfare activism declined.[23] A decade of prosperity, presided over by Calvin Coolidge, rejuvenated individualistic explanations of poverty and reasserted a social Darwinian vision of achievement. When the stock market crashed in 1929, the nation was unprepared. The first reaction was one of silence. Many blamed themselves for their poverty.

> The unemployed worker almost always experienced feelings of guilt and self-depreciation. Although he knew millions had been thrown out of work through no fault of their own, he knew too that millions more were still employed. He could not smother the conviction that his joblessness was the result of his own inadequacy.[24]

Over time, the unemployed came to see that the shared fate of millions would have to be publicly communicated and protested. Reaction began sporadically, and again it was those outside government who took the lead. Breadlines became mobs; looting of food became a "nationwide phenomenon."[25] By 1930 the left had begun systematically to organize the unemployed. Major cities had unemployment marches. Through the year, mass rallies were formed to protest unemployment and to demand public works and relief measures.

One of the most famous organized protest efforts was conducted by the veterans of World War I. After the war, Congress had authorized a bonus to be paid to the veterans in 1945, in compensation for their economic losses during the war. In 1930 the veterans, mostly unemployed and impoverished, demanded their bonuses immediately to tide them over during the crisis. In June 1932, between 15,000 and 20,000 veterans, many with their families, came to Washington to dramatize their needs. Congress eventually paid the veterans half their bonuses, but President Hoover ordered troops to remove the marchers. The *Washington News* observed: "What a pitiable spectacle is that of the Great American Government . . . chasing men, women and children with army tanks. . . . If the Army must be called out to make war on unarmed citizens, this is no longer America."[26]

Through 1932 the crisis deepened. Conditions of unemployment and spiraling deflation intensified. Rent strikes spread, and worker revolts protesting wage cuts broke out in textile mills in Massachusetts, New Jersey, and Pennsylvania. Miners' protests grew violent in Kentucky, Arkansas, Ohio, Indiana, and West Virginia.[27] By the summer of 1932 labor violence had become commonplace throughout the country.

The New Deal

With the election of Franklin Roosevelt in 1932, the inside process joined the rising demand for reform from outside government to create the climate for another period of social welfare expansion. Within months, Roosevelt had closed and then reopened the banks, addressed the problems of agriculture, and initiated the National Industrial Recovery Act, which fostered economic cooperation, affirmed the right of collective bargaining, established a forty-hour week, outlawed child labor, and set a minimum wage.[28]

Over the next few years, the New Deal administration generated the largest package of relief and job-creation programs the country had ever witnessed. The alphabet programs, as they were called, included the Civilian Conservation Corps (CCC), the Federal Emergency Relief Act (FERA), the Public Works Administration (PWA), the Civil Works Administration (CWA), the Works Progress Administration (WPA), and the National Youth Administration (NYA). These programs reemployed millions of workers and distributed temporary relief funds to families across the nation. Building on the demands of those outside government in the pre–New Deal years and continually aware of outside voices that were pressing for more radical change, those inside Roosevelt's administration created hundreds of programs to address the immediate critical needs of the Depression.

These measures, however, were all viewed as temporary, to be phased out as the crisis passed.[29] Of more permanent significance was the Social Security bill, an act that was designed to help prevent such emergencies in the future. The Social Security Act, which was passed in 1935, provided, on a federal level, for old-age and survivors insurance, old-age assistance, aid to dependent children, and aid to the blind. A federal-state formula for unemployment insurance was included as well. A generation of activism by those outside government on behalf of social insurance was reflected in the Social Security Act. It was not perfect: medical measures were omitted, old-age insurance was pegged to previous income levels, and large groups were left uncovered. Nevertheless, Social Security remains the most inclusive and universalistic social welfare program ever passed by the American federal government.[30]

The 1930s constitute a striking amalgam of external and internal processes working to produce social change. The economic crisis of 1929 took the country unaware. The response, slow at first, became a demand for action from outside government. The electoral change produced by a combination of worsening economic conditions and the protests they aroused placed in power an administration prepared to work for the needed reforms. Roosevelt brought into government many who had previously worked outside the system. Social workers and social activists took a leading role in representing the interests of the unemployed. The outcome was a federalized approach to social welfare that still serves as a model for addressing the social problems of an industrial society.

1940–1960: The Pendulum Swings Back Again

The years during World War II were, as might be expected, a time of overpowering concern for events abroad; social welfare was no longer an important issue on the public agenda. Nor did matters change significantly in the years immediately following the war. Like the 1920s, the post–World War II period produced an "affluent" and somewhat conservative America.[31] Radical politics ceased with the onset of McCarthyism, and public concern for domestic social reform subsided.

New demands for social justice, however, were evolving. A new outside process was gathering steam. In 1955, when Rosa Parks refused to move to the back of the bus, the civil rights movement came alive. The Montgomery bus boycott which followed was the first of many strikes, sit-ins, marches, and boycotts bent on defeating Jim Crowism and arousing American sensitivity to the problems of discrimination. The Southern Christian Leadership Conference, under the direction of Rev. Martin Luther King, became perhaps the best known of the civil rights organizations, but it was not the only one. Established organizations, including the NAACP, the Urban League, and the Congress of Racial Equality (CORE), also took an active role, while the Student Non-Violent Coordinating Committee (SNCC) began to produce a new generation of youthful civil rights leaders. Other local, religious, radical, and nationalist organizations joined the cause, including the Mississippi Freedom Democratic Party, the Black Muslims, the Black Panther Party, and the Republic of New Africa.[32]

At the same time, teachers, writers, and scholars were making their own contribution to the outside process. Concerns about juvenile delinquency drew public attention to problems of poverty and urban violence. The need for equal opportunity was advanced by Richard Cloward and Lloyd Ohlin.[33] Michael Harrington and Dwight McDonald were documenting *The Other America* and "Our Invisible Poor."[34] Private organizations, including the Mobilization for Youth and Haryou in New York City and the Ford Foundation's "Gray Areas" project in New Haven, were also beginning to test solutions to problems of poverty and delinquency.[35]

The New Frontier and the Great Society: 1961–1968

The growing agitation outside government for expanded initiatives in social welfare simmered through the 1950s but found a sympathetic ear in the White House by 1960. President Kennedy had been shaken by the widespread poverty he had observed in West Virginia during his campaign; he had read the work of Harrington and McDonald; he recognized Martin Luther King as a leader of both moral and political strength whose demands must be taken into account.

The first three years of the 1960s represented the beginnings of an inside process for the expansion of social welfare. Domestic legislation included the Area Redevelopment Act of 1961, the Manpower Development and Training Act of 1962, the Social Security Act Amendments of 1962, and the Community Mental Health Centers Act of 1963. Attorney General Robert Kennedy headed the President's Committee on Juvenile Delinquency, which established links with various experimental programs that had been developing outside government over the previous years. Work began on legislation to address poverty and chronic unemployment.

Frustrated by their inability to obtain congressional approval for many of their bills, members of the Kennedy administration worked toward establishing that important additional element of an effective inside process, a sympathetic Congress. The mid-term elections of 1962 represented movement in that direction, and more was hoped from 1964. Kennedy and his staff worked for rules changes in the House of Representatives that would facilitate efforts for reform; these were achieved in the summer of 1963.[36]

With Kennedy's assassination in the fall of 1963, it fell to Lyndon Johnson to complete the legislative efforts Kennedy had begun. In his first year in office, Johnson launched the War on Poverty and passed the Civil Rights Act of 1964, two historic social welfare efforts toward which the outside and inside processes had been working for more than a decade. Following his remarkable electoral mandate in 1964, Johnson initiated his Great Society, an avalanche of reforms equaled only by Franklin Roosevelt's first term. Dozens of education bills were passed, Medicare and Medicaid were added to Social Security, a Demonstration Model Cities Program was enacted, voting rights were reaffirmed, and a host of other social welfare programs, many long advocated by those inside or outside government, were established. As Robert Albright observed in the Washington *Post*, the Great Society "brought to harvest a generation's backlog of ideas and social legislation."[37]

But the symbiosis of inside and outside processes that gave birth to the Great Society under Johnson's impressive leadership was short-lived. While advocacy groups complained with increasing stridency that reforms were too slow and tentative, state and municipal leaders objected that they were too sweeping. The outside support for social change was rapidly dissolving.

As the outside processes for reform began to splinter, a more powerful force intervened: the war in Vietnam. As the war absorbed more and more attention from those inside government, as well as more resources, the impetus for social reform melted away. By 1968 the third great period of expansion in American social welfare was over.

THE POLICY PENDULUM AND ITS DYNAMICS

This brief overview of the three periods in which the policy pendulum swung toward social activism suggests how forces outside government interact with those inside to create significant movement in social policy.

Although we have focused our discussion of the inside and outside processes particularly on the periods during which they led to the expansion of social welfare, these processes in fact go on continuously; the contraction and consolidation of social welfare also involve the interaction of those inside and outside government, although the goals and outcomes of such interaction are quite different.

To some extent, the expansion of social welfare requires a more focused effort of the inside and outside processes, because it seeks a more proactive role for government. Four factors influence the expansion of social welfare: (1) the severity of the social problems involved and their public recognition, (2) the strength and acceptability of ideas proposed to alleviate the problems, (3) the cohesion of those involved in the outside process, and (4) the effectiveness and commitment of the inside process. Let us explore how each of these influences the policy pendulum.

Severity and Recognition of Social Problems

It can be argued that social problems such as income maintenance, the need for medical care, unemployment, alcoholism, and child abuse have always existed. Certainly they have been present in all recent periods of American history. Two factors then become important: (1) how severe any one of these problems becomes at a particular time, and (2) to what extent its severity is recognized. As a nation, Americans monitor economic measures, such as employment, inflation, and income, but no systematic and public yardsticks have been developed for the more intangible social problems, such as sickness, mental illness, family distress, or hunger. It is therefore very difficult to know the severity of social problems at a given time. A composite index of national health or social well-being is far from realization.

Because this is true, public action on social problems is likely to take place, not as a result of objective measurement, but because certain problems become dramatized and legitimized through such aspects of the outside process as books, newspapers, television, movies, public education campaigns, and protests. The relationship between a problem's actual existence and its public recognition is a complex one. In 1958, for example, John Kenneth Galbraith's *The Affluent Society* described poverty as if it were disappearing, shrunk to insular pockets in an otherwise prosperous nation.[38] Two years later, Michael Harrington's *The Other America* caused alarm by "rediscovering" the problem of poverty.[39] Of course, little had changed with regard to the actual problem of poverty in those two years, but the level of recognition had been altered. Harrington's work in fact was one of many influences that helped move the Kennedy and Johnson administrations closer toward the War on Poverty.

The existence of a severe social problem, then, is not sufficient stimulus to initiate policy development. Public attention is needed as well, in order for the problem to find its way into the policy process. Building public support for change through the dissemination of information about social problems has been a traditional task of the outside process, but those inside government frequently play a critical role as well. The history of social welfare policy formulation is replete with examples of both, from Jane Addams and Florence Kelley on the outside to Frances Perkins and Harry Hopkins and Eleanor Roosevelt on the inside, from outsiders like Martin Luther King and Ralph Nader to insiders like Hubert Humphrey and Robert Kennedy. All helped dramatize social problems and build support for programs designed to address them.

Strength and Acceptability of Ideas

The recognition of social problems and the awareness of their severity are necessities. But for policy to evolve, the solutions proposed need to be (and to appear to be) sound and acceptable—or at least sufficiently within the potential range of acceptability to gain popular support. As we have noted, the income maintenance programs of the 1930s were ideas that had been discussed for more than forty years before the New Deal. Though dismissed by Americans for several decades as too radical both in principle and design, particularly if a federal role and comprehensive coverage were proposed, the urgency of the Depression created a new environment in which the same ideas proved both acceptable and compelling.

In contrast, we can consider more recent proposals for income maintenance that were less successful. President Nixon's Family Assistance Plan in 1969, candidate George McGovern's ''demo-grant'' proposal in 1972, and President Carter's Program for Better Jobs and Income in 1977 all failed to attract the necessary public enthusiasm. Although throughout these years there was a fair level of consensus that the problem of income maintenance needed addressing, no one of these solutions appeared sufficiently sound and acceptable to gain popular support.

Clearly, a proposal for change must strike the general public as one that is workable, that will improve conditions, and that will not be of greater cost than benefit. If these criteria are not met, no amount of public consensus on the severity of the problem is likely to be sufficient to assure action.

Cohesion of the Outside Process

Another important element in creating conditions that will support social reform is the extent to which those outside government work together for change. Alexis de Tocqueville noted Americans' difficulty with such cooperation as early as 1835: ''No sooner do you set foot on American soil, than you find yourself in a sort of tumult; a confused clamor rises on every side, and a thousand voices are heard at once, each expressing some social requirement.''[40]

Over the years, the ''clamor and tumult'' have intensified. Leary lists some of the issues around which single-interest groups have formed over the past twenty years: civil rights, women's rights, migrant workers, consumer protection, gay rights, fundamentalist religion, right to life, school prayer, anti-pornography, tax revolt, and nuclear freeze.[41] Others she might have added include black power, the aging, the physically disabled, Hispanics, the mentally ill, and Vietnam veterans.

Like the general public, political leaders—members of the inside process—respond less well to fragmented messages from outside government.[42] Confronted by a rapidly multiplying number of groups—each committed to a single issue, unsympathetic to others' claims, and unwilling to compromise—the politician, like the common citizen, is likely either to disregard them all or to respond to those few interests that are presented most forcefully. In either case, the opportunity to develop common themes and common solutions is obscured. Califano argues that this lack of cohesion ''mines the road to progress.'' He adds:

> The proliferation of these groups is an increasing problem, and the difficulty is not simply related to any particular group or ideological bent, whether they are good guys or bad guys, as measured against some political philosophy. Nothing is more appealing than helping people who are physically crippled, but the focus on the handicapped alone, like all one-dimensional views of the world, is too narrow for the formulation of broad policies in the national interest.[43]

Problems of cohesion and coherence in the outside process, then, may result in public confusion, apathy, or backlash, possibly even hurting the cause that is being advocated; they also fail to provide an effective and reasonably stable coalition pressing those inside government for reform. On the other hand, the cohesion, unity, and perseverance of the outside process can, under good conditions, provide a significant portion of the energy by which the policy pendulum moves. When those outside government are willing to work together, they increase their power to heighten public awareness of social problems, to strengthen public faith in proposed solutions, and to set the stage for the further contributions of the inside process.

Effectiveness and Commitment of the Inside Process

All the factors listed above, even when working together in optimal fashion, probably will not generate actual policy change without the effective committed support of those inside government, especially the president. As James MacGregor Burns observes,

> the President has the attention of the country, the administrative goals, the command of information, and the fiscal resources that are necessary for intelligent planning, and he is gaining the institutional power that will make such planning operational. Better than any other human instrumentality, he can order the relations of his ends and means, alter existing institutions and procedures or create new ones, calculate the consequences of different policies, experiment with various methods, control the timing of action, anticipate the reactions of affected interests, and conciliate them or at least mediate among them.[44]

When Burns wrote these words in 1965, the imperial presidency was not yet an idea out of fashion. But even now, with the office's luster dimmed by Vietnam, Watergate, and two decades of diminishing faith in the charismatic leader who will solve all our problems, there is no other individual in the country with a remotely comparable potential for unifying the energies of the country toward a single purpose. Leadership from inside government depends, as we have noted, on preparatory work from the outside process. "A president so far ahead of his time as to voice aspirations the common man is not yet ready to understand," writes Harold Laski, "is inevitably doomed to failure. The kind of challenge, this is to say, which he must make is one for which history has prepared a wide and secure foundation."[45] Doris Kearns, writing of President Johnson, concurs: "Political leaders in a democracy are not revolutionaries or leaders of creative thought. The best of them are those who respond wisely to changes and movements already under way."[46]

The test of the inside process, then, is its ability to draw ideas from all sources—inside and outside government—and convert them into practical policies and programs. Burns describes two types of leadership that are essential to this process: "transactional" and "transformational."[47] Transactional leaders, he says, "make short-run plans, adjust to others' needs and decisions, adapt their hopes and aspirations to existing conditions, bargain and compete and maneuver in a continuing series of accommodations."[48] Transformational leaders, on the other hand, see beyond their constituents' immediate demands and seek to build programs that address the deeper hopes and aspirations beneath, hopes and aspirations that link to a more fundamental commonality among multiple groups and constituencies. While Burns expresses a clear preference for the second form of leadership, history suggests that both are essential in order to achieve significant social change. The inside process is most successful when those in government handle the transactional aspect of policymaking with sophistication and skill, while recognizing and responding as well to the obligation for transformational leadership.

We have reviewed four factors that influence the swing of the policy pendulum: the severity and recognition of social problems, the feasibility of proposed solutions, the coherence of the outside process, and the effectiveness and commitment of the inside process. It is the interaction of these four factors that helps move the policy pendulum from periods of contraction in social welfare to periods of expansion.

THE SOCIAL WELFARE INSTITUTION

Generalizations about history and its dynamics are, of course, open to argument and refinement. Such references to the past are necessary, however, in order to develop a clearer picture of the current social welfare institution and of its possible direction. One observation does seem apparent and important. During the Progressive Era, there was no social welfare institution on a national, public level. The work of social reformers during that time was, in a sense, from the "bottom up." They could point to appalling conditions and propose new ideas without having to defend an existing structure of programs and policies. The same was true in the 1930s. The framers of the New Deal could, for the most part, conceive and implement policy and program on a national level with a *tabula rasa*—a clean slate—on which to work. By the 1960s this was less the case, and by the end of that decade it was not so at all. Bureaucracies, constituencies, and the accompanying skepticism about both were firmly in place.

This is the environment in which those who have advocated for social welfare change in more recent times have had to make their case. It is no longer practical to imagine a wholly new national approach to social welfare. Whatever changes are initiated must evolve from present systems. What is needed, then, is an analysis of the social welfare institution as it exists today; this must precede any considerations for reform and change. Efforts toward a new swing of the pendulum must of necessity begin with the complex social welfare institution that now exists.

In the next three chapters we will examine three elements that interact to influence the shape of social welfare as an institution—values, technology, and structure. These are by no means the only important elements, but we contend that they are vital in determining the nature of social welfare.[49] Values, technology, and structure will provide in Part I a framework for analysis of the institution. In Part II we will apply this framework to the actual functioning of the institution in order to explore certain patterns and trends that we feel are important to an understanding of social welfare today. Finally, Part III will identify some possible directions for future change, based on our analysis.

SUMMARY

This chapter began with an introduction of the concept of the policy pendulum, which has swung in different periods of American history toward or away from the expansion of social welfare. Three periods of significant expansion were identified: the Progressive Era (1900–1918), the New Deal (1933–1938), and the New Frontier/Great Society (1960–1968).

Two processes, one outside government, one inside, interact to move the policy pendulum. The outside process includes those with social problems and those who speak on their behalf—scholars, journalists, and other concerned citizens, cooperating to articulate social issues. Inside government, a complementary process goes on, converting public concern into policies and programs. In order for the inside and outside processes to move social welfare in the direction of expansion, four factors are necessary: public recognition of severe social problems, feasible proposals for their solution, a cohesive and coherent outside process, and an effective and sympathetic inside process.

NOTES

1. Arthur S. Link, ed., *The Papers of Woodrow Wilson*, vol. 27 (Princeton: Princeton University Press, 1978), p. 150.

2. Samuel Rosenman, ed., *The Public Papers and Addresses of Franklin Delano Roosevelt*, vol. 3 (New York: Random House, 1938), p. 288.

3. Herbert Hoover, *The New Day: Campaign Speeches of Herbert Hoover* (Stanford, Calif.: Stanford University Press, 1929), p. 168.

4. Dwight D. Eisenhower, *Public Papers of the United States Presidents: 1957* (Washington, D.C.: U.S. Government Printing Office, 1958), p. 759.

5. Barbara Ward, *The Home of Man* (New York: W. W. Norton & Company, 1976), p. 250.

6. See Frances Fox Piven and Richard Cloward, *Poor People's Movements* (New York: Random House, 1977).

7. There are several important works in the history of social welfare that provide more detail on these periods. One is Walter Trattner, *From Poor Law to Welfare State* (New York: Free Press, 1974); another is Samuel Mencher, *Poor Law to Poverty Program* (Pittsburgh: University of Pittsburgh Press, 1967). For a historical thesis about the development of social welfare, see Piven and Cloward, *Regulating the Poor* (New York, Vintage Press, 1971).

8. See, for example, Trattner, *From Poor Law to Welfare State*, chap. 8.

9. Gerald Handel, *Social Welfare in Western Society* (New York: Random House, 1982), pp. 72, 75.

10. June Axinn and Herman Levin, *Social Welfare: A History of the American Response to Need* (New York: Dodd, Mead and Co., 1975), p. 132.

11. Fred M. Cox and Charles Garvin, "Community Organization Practice: 1865-1973," in *Strategies of Community Organization*, ed. Fred M. Cox et al. (Itaska, Ill.: F. E. Peacock Publishers, Inc., 1974), pp. 43-44.

12. Trattner, *From Poor Law to Welfare State*, p. 148.

13. See Allen F. Davis, *Spearheads for Reform, The Social Settlements and the Progressive Era* (New York: Oxford University Press, 1967), pp. 9, 12.

14. Christopher Lasch, ed., *The Social Thought of Jane Addams* (New York: Bobbs-Merrill Co., 1965), p. xx.

15. Axinn and Levin, *Social Welfare*, pp. 127, 131, 132.

16. Lela B. Costin, *Child Welfare: Policies and Practice* (New York: McGraw Hill Book Co., 1972), p. 12.

17. Grace Abbott, *The Child and the State* (Chicago: University of Chicago Press, 1938), pp. 495-506. See also Daniel Levine, *Jane Addams and the Liberal Tradition* (Madison, Wis.: State Historical Society of Wisconsin, 1971).

18. Mencher, *Poor Law to Poverty Program* (Pittsburgh: University of Pittsburgh Press, 1967), p. 302. See also Cox and Garvin, "Community Organization Practice," p. 45.

19. Axinn and Levin, *Social Welfare*, pp. 125-126.

20. Cox and Garvin, "Community Organization Practice," pp. 45-46.

21. William L. O'Neill, *The Progressive Years: America Comes of Age* (New York: Harper & Row, 1975), p. 65.

22. Davis, *Spearheads for Reform*, p. 198.

23. Trattner, *From Poor Law to Welfare State*, pp. 151, 153.

24. William Leuchtenberg, *Franklin D. Roosevelt and the New Deal* (New York: Harper Colophon Books, 1963), pp. 118-119.

25. Piven and Cloward, *Poor People's Movements*, p. 49.

26. Arthur M. Schlesinger, *The Crisis of the Old Order, 1919-1933* (Boston: Houghton Mifflin, 1957), p. 265.

27. Piven and Cloward, *Poor People's Movements*, p. 109.

28. Axinn and Levin, *Social Welfare*, p. 171.

29. Arthur Schlesinger, *The Coming of the New Deal* (Boston: Houghton Mifflin, 1958).

30. Leuchtenberg, *Roosevelt and the New Deal*, pp. 132-133. See also Thomas M. Meenaghan and Robert O. Washington, *Social Policy and Social Welfare* (New York: Free Press, 1980), chap. 10.

31. John Kenneth Galbraith, *The Affluent Society* (New York, The New American Library, 1958).

32. Cox and Garvin, "Community Organization Practice," pp. 53-54.

33. Richard Cloward and Lloyd Ohlin, *Delinquency and Opportunity* (Glencoe, Ill.: Free Press, 1960).

34. See Michael Harrington, *The Other America: Poverty in the United States* (New York: Macmillan Company, 1962); Dwight MacDonald, "Our Invisible Poor," *New Yorker*, Jan. 19, 1963.

35. John C. Donovan, *The Politics of Poverty* (New York: Pegasus, 1967).

36. Lewis J. Paper, *The Promise and the Performance: The Leadership of John F. Kennedy* (New York: Crown Publishers, 1975), pp. 257-259.

37. James L. Sundquist, *Politics and Policy: The Eisenhower, Kennedy and Johnson Years* (Washington, D.C.: Brookings Institution, 1968), p. 2.

38. Galbraith, *The Affluent Society*.

39. Harrington, *The Other America*.

40. Alexis de Tocqueville, *Democracy in America* (New York: Anchor Books, 1969), vol. 1, p. 242.

41. Mary Ellen Leary, "The Movements Are Here to Stay," in Walter Truett Anderson, ed., *Rethinking Liberalism* (New York: Avon Books, 1983), p. 221.

42. For a discussion of the tension between single-interest groups' approach and the American political system's need for compromise, see Lawrence D. Brown, *New Policies, New Politics: Government's Response to Government's Growth, a Staff Paper* (Washington, D.C.: Brookings Institution, 1983), pp. 39-46; Clinton Rossiter, *Parties and Politics in America* (New York: New American Library, 1960), pp. 29-32, 69-72.

43. Joseph A. Califano, Jr., *Governing America: An Insider's Report from the White House and the Cabinet* (New York: Simon and Schuster, 1981), p. 450.

44. James M. Burns, *Presidential Government* (New York: Avon Books, 1965), pp. 326-327.

45. Harold Laski, *The American Presidency, an Interpretation* (New York: Harper & Brothers Publishers, 1940), p. 269.

46. Doris Kearns, *Lyndon Johnson and the American Dream* (New York: Harper & Row), 1976, p. 211.

47. James MacGregor Burns, *The Power to Lead: The Crisis of the American Presidency* (New York: Simon & Schuster, 1984).

48. Ibid., p. 153.

49. There has been much important work on the nature and state of social welfare as an institution. Such works as Richard Titmuss, *Commitment to Welfare* (London: Allen and Unwin, 1968) and *Social Policy* (London: Allen and Unwin, 1974) have become classics and have significantly influenced the conceptual development of this book. Other works in a similar category are Harold Wilensky and Charles Lebeaux, *Industrial Society and Social Welfare* (New York: Free Press, 1958), and T. H. Marshall, *Social Policy* (London: Hutchinson, 1965). Some more recent books of enormous help have been Meenaghan and Washington, *Social Policy and Social Welfare* (New York: Free Press, 1980); Norman Furniss and Timothy Tilton, *The Case for the Welfare State* (Bloomington, Ind.: Indiana University Press, 1977); Robert Pinker, *The Idea of Welfare* (London: Heinemann, 1979).

CHAPTER TWO

How Values
Shape
Social Welfare

The relationship of values and societal institutions is two-directional. Values influence the nature and form of institutions, and institutions, as they change and evolve, help reshape values. To analyze an important American institution such as the family or religion is to understand something significant about the society's system of values; to analyze an important value, such as individualism, is to learn more about the dynamics of society's institutions. The concept of value is an elusive one. Values are difficult to concretize and measure, and they vary from the obvious to the obscure. They are always in a state of change: Sometimes they merge to form coherent systems, sometimes they have vague relationships, often they are in conflict. It is difficult to generalize about values and to maintain, for example, that the society as a whole holds one set of values rather than another. The values of particular groups may be influenced by occupation, race, age, class position, or such external factors as changing economic conditions and new norms of social behavior.

It is also apparent that no in-depth analysis of American social welfare can escape a consideration of values. When one begins to explore social welfare, questions of value become central. Issues of equality, social justice, compassion, liberty, freedom of choice, social control, social conflict, and redistribution are but a few examples of the close link between values and social policy. It is apparent, from the mere mention of these few issues, that public debate about social welfare can be expected to draw on emotions and convictions as much as on logical argument. Facts take one only so far. Hence, the nature of certain American values, their consistencies and contradictions, provide an important entry point for the analysis of social welfare.

This chapter will, of course, be selective. No claim can be made that all values relevant to an understanding of social welfare will be considered. Those chosen, however, seem of central importance because they are values that appear to play particularly significant roles in influencing Americans' attitudes and actions in the area of social welfare.

Social Well-Being: A Consensual Value

To this point, the term "social welfare" has been used to mean a social institution composed of certain programs and policies. The term can, in fact, be more broadly defined as the sum total of resources, policies, programs, and technical knowledge devoted by society to the pursuit of optimal social conditions. This definition suggests a further meaning of social welfare that is vital to any discussion of its relationship to American values. Social welfare can be viewed as a terminal value, as an end-in-itself, simply the welfare of those in the society. From this perspective, a clear and perhaps universal consensus about social welfare does indeed exist; it is not difficult to reach agreement that life, liberty, and the pursuit of happiness are general and shared values. Most, if not all, of the people in our society place a high value on proper medical care, economic security, decent housing, adequate clothing, and conditions in which the more intangible goals such as feelings of satisfaction and well-being can at least be pursued. These values can be inferred from our behavior as well as assumed from our stated beliefs. They appear in many of our society's official documents—the laws that charter our human service organizations, the platforms of our political parties, and the Constitution itself. Social welfare conceived in this way finds few outspoken adversaries. The problem, of course, arises when the means to achieve this social welfare are considered.

It is important to distinguish between the two meanings. For purposes of clarity, the term "social well-being" will be used to denote the consensual value, and "social welfare" will be used to refer to the societal institution designed to facilitate social well-being. It is important to note, therefore, that social well-being is an important underlying value of social welfare. It does not appear extreme to contend that it is, in fact, a major driving force. The fundamental intent of social welfare—to improve the general social well-being—has generally received widespread support. Opinion polls, for instance, usually report high levels of public approval for the intent of social welfare. When questions such as "Should the government do more to help the poor in this country?" are posed, the response is consistently affirmative. On the other hand, if the question "Should the government increase welfare benefits?" is asked, the response is generally quite different.[1] Again, there is a distinction between ends and means, between philosophy and program, between a concern for social well-being and support for social welfare as an institution. Nevertheless, it does appear that at the level of personal values most Americans share a commitment to the social well-being of the overall community.

Besides this commitment to social well-being, Americans share a number of other values that help shape their attitudes toward social welfare. Some are held widely, and some are especially strong in particular regions, cultures, or social classes. But among those that appear to have meaning for a broad cross section of the American people, two clusters can be identified that have particular relevance for our discussion of social welfare.

One cluster, which we have termed "traditional values," includes the principles of self-reliance, individualism, choice, efficiency, productivity, and competition. These values, emphasizing what each individual can do for himself, place relatively minor importance on mutual assistance and support.

Softening these traditional values is a set of "temporizing values," including compassion, service, equality of opportunity, participation, and fairness. These principles are more directly associated with social intervention, stressing as they do the obligations of mutual concern through which members of a society support each other.

In this chapter we will discuss first the traditional values and then the temporizing values. We will conclude by examining the implications of both clusters for the shape of social welfare.

TRADITIONAL VALUES

Self-Reliance, Individualism, and Choice

Three deeply held beliefs hold a special place in the American system of values: self-reliance, individualism, and choice. Because of their importance, they are essential to an understanding of the American social welfare institution. Deep in the philosophical roots of this country is the idea that, in the final analysis, the individual is responsible for his or her own destiny. Such a notion is derived from a mélange of ideas and traditions. One is the so-called Protestant ethic. In ideal form, the Protestant ethic offers a model for individual behavior. One must be hardworking, God-fearing, disciplined, goal-oriented, frugal, and willing to defer the pleasures of the moment for the sake of well-earned long-term rewards and satisfactions. Although the term ''Protestant ethic'' has its roots in the Puritan and Calvinistic tradition, its substance is shared by other segments of American society and by the traditions of other cultures as well.

One element in the American tradition that has reinforced the values of self-reliance and individualism is the real and symbolic notion of a frontier, with its promise (to use a more recent term) of upward mobility. ''In the United States,'' Gertrude Stein observed, ''there is more space where nobody is than where anybody is. This is what makes America what it is.'' [2] This tradition of open land and open opportunity tended to reinforce Americans' belief in individualism and self-reliance. The frontier could best be cultivated through the initiative and effort of many enterprising individuals, which in turn would produce the best possible outcome for the individuals, their families, and the nation. The frontier meant that there was no need for dependency, that each person could rise in society and make a better life through his or her own talent and skill.

Implicit in the idea of the frontier was the notion of expansion. The most industrious would strive for continuous expansion, which would benefit everyone. Future benefits for the community as a whole would come, not from the redistribution of current resources, but from the expanding pool of resources generated through individual initiative. In this sense, individuals' efforts to improve their own lots were seen as serving the public as well, since they contributed to the nation's overall prosperity.

Given the existence of a frontier and an abundance of individual initiative to exploit it, and given that the resulting growth and expansion would be of benefit to all, the only potential impediment was some outside force that would intervene to prevent individuals from capitalizing on available opportunities. The individual must remain unshackled, free to pursue the chances that presented themselves. Hence, freedom of choice became an important complement to self-reliance and individualism in the American value system. If there was a comfort in knowing that one could depend on one's own talents and skills, the allied fear was that some force imposed from the outside would hinder their full use. Only through freedom and choice would true self-reliance and individualism be achieved.

The classic argument for free choice is derived from the political and economic concept of *laissez faire*.[3] Originally expounded in the writings of Adam Smith, the theory holds that there is a natural economic order, which, left unfettered, will bring about the most good for the greatest number.[4] John Stuart Mill's essay *On Liberty* offered a similar view of the political arena: ''The only freedom which deserves the name is that of pursuing our own good in our own way, so long as we do not attempt to deprive others of theirs or impede their efforts to attain it.''[5] It is obvious that this ideology, which has survived and prospered in America, fits very well with the idea of frontier and expansion. It has been a driving force in the American value system and maintains a numerous and perhaps growing corps of advocates today.

The values of self-reliance, individualism, and free choice have important implications for the less fortunate members of society. Clearly, some are less industrious, less productive, and less responsible than others; they contribute less to the overall expansion and general good of society. What factors can explain this deviancy from generally held and favored values? One explanation that has continued to command a following was first popularized by Herbert Spencer as ''social Darwinism.'' By applying Darwin's principles regarding the ''survival of the fittest'' to social conditions, Spencer and his successors argued that poverty and other forms of social deprivation are primarily caused by the victims' own ''unfitness.''[6] Those who prosper, according to this argument, are by definition those whom nature intended for prosperity. No intervention on behalf of the unsuccessful can significantly change their lot, since they are primarily the victims not of social structures, but of a naturally ordained system of competition.

Much has been written about the relationship of social Darwinism to American thought and ideology in such areas as economics, population policy, and eugenics.[7] What is central for our purposes is that according to Spencer's formulation social problems are primarily attributable to deficiencies of individuals, characteristics that can lead to temporary or permanent dependency on the rest of society. This viewpoint sometimes leads to arguments for continuing charitable assistance; at other times it has been used to justify ruthless indifference. This is a subject to which we will return in later chapters. But whichever policy direction results, the fundamental value orientation is that self-reliance is the normal condition, whereas dependency of any kind can be seen as an indication of individual failure.

Efficiency, Productivity, and Competition

Closely related to the traditional values of self-reliance, individualism, and free choice are those of efficiency, productivity, and competition. These three values serve to form an important element of the American value system.

Benjamin Franklin captured the American philosophy as early as 1784: "Here people do not enquire concerning a stranger, What is he? but What can he do? If he has any useful art, he is welcome. . . ." The productive, the efficient, and the competitive understand and practice an important formula: Profit equals investment minus cost $(P = I - C)$. This is "the bottom line" that runs American private enterprise, from the huge corporation to the small business. It guides the seller and the buyer. It constitutes the guiding and natural laws described by Adam Smith and reflects the fundamental notion of our economic theories of supply and demand.

Smith and his followers argued that individuals will, if left unfettered, act and work to maximize this formula; the result, they maintained, will be of benefit to the individuals themselves and through systems of exchange, to society as a whole. They will act in their own self-interest, and that self-interest will serve the interest of all. A precise understanding of the nature of profit, investment, and cost, as well as a pragmatic application of that knowledge, brings the most efficient, the most competitive, and ultimately the most productive approach to all forms of human exchange.

This equation is not confined in its application to exchanges of money and goods. It has found its way into other aspects of our thought and action. Behaviorist psychology suggests a social equivalent to the "bottom line," with its focus on the relationship between rewards and punishments for various actions and the way in which such actions form patterns of behavior perceived profitable to the individual. Exchange theory, which contains many of the same elements as supply-and-demand economics and behaviorist psychology, has had a profound influence on American sociology.[8] It argues that individuals and groups relate on the basis of how they assess the probable investments, costs, and rewards of particular interactions. Hence, the cohesion or duration of a group or community is based on its ability to generate rewards in exchange for each individual's continued participation. Recent and more popularized versions of these approaches can be found in transactional analysis and game theory.

Productivity, efficiency, and competition can be viewed as desirable for their own sake. Efficiency promulgates order, care, moderation, and responsibility, and it guards against excess. Productivity in our society is expected to lead to esteem, self-worth, satisfaction, security, social sanction, and prestige.

Competition, too, is valued; many feel it can bring out individual capacities that may not emerge under other conditions. The keenness of the struggle is often thought to be as important as the result; freedom to compete means the freedom to advance and to prosper.

These, then, are some of the traditional values that have helped shape Americans' approach to social welfare. More than anything else, they stress the individuals' power—and even obligation—to seize their own opportunities, solve their own problems, and shape their own destinies. But there is more to life than individual achievement. As Albert Einstein so eloquently observed:

> Man is, at one and the same time, a solitary being and a social being. As a solitary being, he attempts to protect his own existence and that of those who are closest to him, to satisfy his personal desires, and to develop his innate abilities. As a social being, he seeks to gain the recognition of his fellow human beings, to share in their pleasures, to comfort them in their sorrows, and to improve their conditions of life.[9]

Traditional values such as those described here do not stand alone in the American value system. Their force is temporized by another set of values that focus much more closely on human interaction and mutual support.

TEMPORIZING VALUES

Compassion, Service, and Equality of Opportunity

Josephine Shaw Lowell, of the Charity Organization Society, an avowed self-determinist, had to admit after the 1893 recession that the people's economic problems "were as much beyond their power to avert as if they had been natural calamities of fire, flood or storm."[10] From attitudes such as Lowell's spring what we have termed "temporizing values."

One important value in this cluster is compassion—a concern for fellow beings, particularly those who are less well off. Compassion may be expressed through religion, professional service, or simple neighborliness. If a person is disabled or poor or at a disadvantage of some kind, considerations of compassion urge us to help, at least to the point where the traditional values of self-reliance can be restored. If a person is encumbered to the point where he is unable to help himself, if *laissez faire* seems too harsh, then compassion may surface, and with it the need to act in behalf of others.

The point of balance between temporizing values like compassion and other more traditional values has always been the question of how much compassion can be afforded before the traditional values begin to erode, before self-reliance and competition, for example, are threatened. Particularly in America this has represented a continuing source of tension to the interaction between traditional values like self-reliance and temporizing values like compassion. Nevertheless, compassion has continued to hold its important place in the American value system.

The idea of service is compassion put into action. It has often been perceived as a necessity for those in need; at the same time it has been seen as something that those who do have the necessary characteristics are obligated to provide. Organized private charity, first established in America in the latter part of the nineteenth century, was very much in this mold. Influenced by religious tenets and the need to spread morality and help develop character, early notions of service assumed the form of the charity organization society and "friendly visitation" to the poor. The service itself at that time consisted of providing some financial assistance and food but focused principally on attempts at character building. The fundamental concept was that those who had the appropriate commitment to traditional values could serve as a model for those who did not. The poor of the time, like the mentally ill, were viewed as people who, because of their disabilities, could not compete and be productive in society. The goal of service to these disabled people was to offer temporary help, which would be discontinued as soon as self-reliance was restored and dependency ended.

Gradually, as the nineteenth century gave way to the twentieth, the concept of service based on the personal obligation of the advantaged was expanded to include a broader view of social commitment. True service to the victims of social problems, it began to be seen, must involve more than episodic gifts and visits. As Jane Addams wrote: "To attain individual morality in an age demanding social morality, to pride one's self on the results of personal effort when the time demands social adjustment, is utterly to fail to apprehend the situation."[11]

As this broader definition of service gained support, it grew to include a wide range of efforts to improve social conditions, to effect social change, and to build institutions that would provide assistance as a matter of public policy rather than as a form of charity. Government's role was expanded and soon became an important element in the provision of service. "Now it is accepted," wrote Eleanor Roosevelt, "that the government has an obligation to guard the rights of an individual so carefully that he never reaches a point at which he needs charity."[12] Thus, the value of service, originally interpreted in strictly personal terms, was now broadened to include efforts through a whole system of social welfare to meet the needs of the disadvantaged.

The value-based belief in service has been joined by another deeply held value, equality of opportunity. Thomas Wolfe gave poetic voice to this value:

To every man his chance, to every man regardless of his birth, his shining golden opportunity—to every man, the right to live, to work, to be himself and to become whatever thing his manhood and his wisdom can combine to make him—this . . . is the promise of America.[13]

In earlier years, equality of opportunity was considered an implicit part of the American experience. According to the American Dream, one immigrant arriving in New York or one family traveling west had as much chance as the next to achieve success. The opportunity was there; the rest was up to them.

In more recent times, the nation's perception of this value has altered. One symbol of the change was Frederick Jackson Turner's famous announcement to the American Historical Association in 1893 that the American frontier had closed.[14] While opinions might differ about the literal accuracy of this statement, it dramatized a larger truth: that the openness of an earlier America was diminishing, to be replaced by markedly increased concentrations of political, social, and economic power. Equality of opportunity was no longer a given in American society.

These changed circumstances led to a new emphasis on the need to ensure through public policy that opportunity remained equal. Over the years there has been broader acceptance of the idea that some people or groups indeed possess the traits specified by traditional values—self-reliance, efficiency, and productivity, for instance. Yet, through no fault of their own, they have not had the opportunity to benefit from them. Equality of opportunity has thus become well established as an American value.

It is important at this point to distinguish between equality of *opportunity*, which Americans have historically valued, and equality of *outcome*, for which they have shown considerable ambivalence. In his visit to America in 1835, Alexis de Tocqueville believed that he saw a commitment to equality of outcome: "The more I advanced in the study of American society, the more I perceived that . . . equality of condition is the fundamental fact from which all others seem to be derived and the central point at which all my observations terminated."[15] Whether or not de Tocqueville's interpretation was accurate at the time, it is certainly true that commitment to equality of condition (or outcome) has not been a predominant feature of the American value system in recent years. Some efforts to redistribute funds from the wealthier to the poorer segments of society have been undertaken (most notably the progressive income tax adopted early in the twentieth century). These, however, have played a relatively small role in the overall improvement of conditions for the poor compared to the effect of a rising standard of living for the nation as a whole. It has been general prosperity, rather than redistribution, that has bettered social conditions for the disadvantaged, leaving them significantly better off than their parents but about as far from the middle class as they were before, since the middle class had also improved in comparison to their own parents.[16]

American values, then, have not placed primary emphasis on equality of condition, but on equality of opportunity. It is the race, not the results, that they expect to be fair. True to their traditional values, they envision a system in which individuals are given equal chances to compete; the outcome can then depend on each individual's own ability, energy, and effort. In this way, the commitment to equal opportunity temporizes but does not erase the commitment to individual achievement.

Participation and Fairness

Despite deeply held convictions about individualism, people do work together in neighborhoods, towns, and cities, as well as in the country as a whole. Agreed-upon structures and processes are necessary to bring this about. American values dictate that people should join together in associations, but that the joining should be voluntary and the process pluralistic. Thus, participation is a deeply held value, embodying free choice and reflecting the traditions of the country. Participation should not be coerced; its particular significance is based in part on its voluntary quality.[17]

Citizens' participation in the development of their own communities has always been viewed as especially vital.[18] The individual volunteering time in governmental or private service is the keystone on which the democratic process of the country is seen to rest. The citizen-politician is the ideal; the careerist-politician is viewed with suspicion. Participation is the heart of pluralism. The motto of the United States expresses a basic belief in pluralism: "Out of many, one"; that many diverse and conflicting viewpoints and interests should be represented, and through their ultimate accommodations, the best decision reached.

Implicit in the notion of pluralism is the idea that temporary coalitions of like interest will form around key issues and questions of concern. Group A will be aligned with Group B around an interest that they share and will temporarily oppose Groups C and D. Yet on a different concern, A and D will find themselves in opposition to B and C. Hence, power does not remain with one group or a given combination of groups, but, in effect, "moves around" as issues change. Pluralism, then, encourages checks and balances against the accumulation of power by any one group or sector of society.[19] As such it is highly valued because it is seen as a safeguard of democracy. Pluralism is a natural process, where interests can be pursued and individuals protected because there is no permanent minority or majority. The obvious and continuing disenfranchisement of particular groups (recently acquiring the term "minorities") is generally viewed as being against the principles of pluralism. "Powerlessness" can be attributed to a lack of equality of opportunity; it means that power is distributed unequally. If some are powerless, others are powerful; as a permanent state of things, this situation can be viewed as alien to the accepted norms of pluralism and participation.

Closely linked to the value of participation is that of fairness, another value that temporizes the harsher traditional values. Sojourner Truth, a woman and a black, put it simply: "We do as much, we eat as much, we want as much."[20] The temporizing values of compassion for the disadvantaged, service to alleviate misfortune, and especially equality of opportunity have served to perpetuate the idea of America as the country above all others where neither birth nor money nor privilege limits one's right to justice. Nearly all the struggles for rights and recognition in the past century—women's suffrage, the labor movement, civil rights, gay rights, access for the handicapped, the Equal Rights Amendment—have drawn a large part of their force from the shared ideal that Americans deserve fair and equal treatment in national life.

But there is a critical difference between equal opportunity and a fair outcome. For instance, if candidates enter a competition with unequal preparation, their ability to profit from equal opportunity will be different. It was recognition of this dilemma that set the stage for the nation's struggle with affirmative action and a more proactive approach to civil rights. The Supreme Court decision on *Brown v. Board of Education* in 1954 broke the first ground with its dictum that "separate but equal" school facilities could not in fact be equal. Action in the areas of employment and housing followed. For the first time, processes were judged unfair not because of how they were undertaken but because they produced unequal results. The effort to reach consensus on what "fairness" means in American life is a continuing one, not settled by the numerous decisions calling for affirmative action in the 1970s or the present trend to disavow these decisions in the 1980s. But the intensity of the debate and the sincerity of protagonists on both sides of the argument suggest the seriousness with which this value of "fairness" is held in American thought.

Participation can contribute in some ways to fairness. If there is widespread participation in the process of decision making, each group has at least the possibility of gaining a fair share in the outcome. It is for this reason that numerous minority groups have sought to increase public awareness of the extent to which they have been denied participation in the social, political, and economic structures of national life. They clearly believe that greater participation will enhance their ability to increase fairness and equal opportunity as well.

We have discussed two clusters of values: traditional (including self-reliance, individualism, choice, efficiency, productivity, and competition) and temporizing (including compassion, service, equality of opportunity, participation, and fairness). Let us move now to the implications of these value clusters for policy choices in the field of social welfare.

VALUES AND THE DEGREE OF SOCIAL INTERVENTION

The issue that most affects the expansion or contraction of the social welfare institution is not whether people believe in or even enunciate either of the value clusters we have described; it is, rather, what actions are proposed toward the realization of these values. Many Americans believe, at least to some extent, in both value clusters. Their approach to social welfare, however, tends to be influenced by which cluster predominates in their thinking. Stronger commitment to temporizing values, for instance, is likely to show itself in stronger support for social intervention as a way of expressing compassion, providing service, enhancing equality of opportunity, expanding participation, and ensuring fairness. Greater adherence to traditional values, on the other hand, is frequently associated with a desire to keep social intervention to a minimum, the theory being that a *laissez-faire* approach is more conducive to self-reliance, individualism, free choice, efficiency, productivity, and competition. Hence, one important aspect of American values in connection with social welfare is their tendency to favor the expansion or restriction of social intervention.

In Chapter One we discussed the periods of expansion and contraction in social welfare that have occurred in this century. These periodic swings of the pendulum can be seen as reflecting a change in the extent to which temporizing or traditional values influenced public opinion about social problems and a corresponding willingness or unwillingness to support social intervention in the realization of those values. Obviously, as we presented in the preceding chapter, the periods of expansion—the Progressive Era, the New Deal, and the Great Society—each represented times of social intervention; the periods in between did not.

The issue of the degree of social intervention is a vital one in the analysis of present-day social welfare as well. It can be argued that despite the more conservative administrations of Nixon, Ford, and Carter—who asserted traditional values, called for less government and reduced and consolidated social welfare—the machinery of social intervention initiated during the Progressive Era, firmly established during the New Deal, and extended during the Great Society, remained largely untouched through the 1970s. Yet social welfare as an instrument of temporizing values by no means survived undamaged. Classic conservative principles were regularly advanced by Barry Goldwater and other political leaders, as well as by prominent economists, including Milton Friedman.[21] Though they did not advocate a total abandonment of social intervention (indeed Friedman was an early advocate for a federal guaranteed national annual income),[22] they put forth a vision of simplified government, less bureaucracy, and the free market[23] that was closely linked to the ideals expressed in traditional values.

With the advent of the Reagan administration, more forceful versions of noninterventionism emerged, again supported by the principles of self-reliance, individualism, and free choice. Social welfare programs were significantly reduced, and individual self-sufficiency again became a guiding principle of national life. So, in this most recent period as in the past, it is possible to identify an association between temporizing values and the expansion of social welfare, alternating periodically with a period during which traditional values re-emerge and social intervention is curtailed.

VALUES AND THE SHAPE OF SOCIAL WELFARE

The values of self-reliance, individualism, choice, productivity, efficiency, competition, compassion, service, equality of opportunity, fairness, and participation have all contributed to the shape and direction of American social welfare. This can be seen, as we will show in Part II, in the kinds of policies and programs that have developed and in the way they have fared in the light of public scrutiny. Obviously, social welfare policies are not directly created by the population at large. But basic program concepts are proposed and implemented in the context of anticipated popular reaction. Usually policies are not too far behind or too far ahead of what is perceived to be generally acceptable.

As we have shown, expansion of the social welfare institution has generally tended to occur at times when temporizing values have gained influence, whereas periods of contraction in social welfare have frequently coincided with the predominance of traditional values. This pattern, however, is sometimes obscured by advocates' choice of language. Often proponents of social welfare will use such traditional values as self-reliance and freedom of choice to argue for social welfare expansion, while those who oppose social programs will stress their commitment to compassion or equal opportunity. Both, as we have noted, will claim that their approach is the way to the achievement of a general state of social well-being.

Rhetoric aside, what appears crucial is the degree to which social intervention is advocated and supported at a given time. This issue, we believe, is one helpful indicator for assessing the relative predominance of temporizing or traditional values during a given period. It is through this tendency to expand or contract the social welfare institution that values are most likely to express themselves in relation to social issues, a tendency that has fundamental impact on the shape and vitality of the social welfare institution.

SUMMARY

In this chapter we discussed values, one of three critical elements that influence the shape of American social welfare. Two meanings of the term "social welfare" were discussed, one representing a general state of social well-being, the second describing the system of policies and programs designed to achieve social well-being. Whereas attitudes toward the latter vary, commitment to the former—social well-being—is a strong and shared value among many Americans.

Other values with important implications for the shape of social welfare were discussed. These were grouped in two clusters: traditional and temporizing. Traditional values, which include self-reliance, individualism, choice, efficiency, productivity, and competition, were described as focusing primarily on the individual's ability to achieve success and satisfaction on his or her own. Temporizing values, which include compassion, service, equality of opportunity, participation, and fairness, place more emphasis on need for mutual support and assistance among members of a society.

Temporizing values, it was shown, tend to be associated with the expansion of social welfare and a generally favorable attitude toward social intervention. Traditional values tend to stress limiting the growth of the social welfare institution and keeping social intervention to a minimum. The balance between these tendencies can be identified in various periods of the past; in later chapters it will be discussed in relation to our own time.

NOTES

1. *The Gallup Poll—Public Opinion 1980*, Scholarly Resources, Inc., Wilmington, Del.

2. Gertrude Stein, *The Geographical History of America, or The Relation of Human Nature to the Human Mind* (New York: Random House, 1936), p. 17.

3. Adam Smith, *The Wealth of Nations* (New York: Modern Library, 1937).

4. Ibid.

5. John Stuart Mill, *On Liberty* (London: Penguin Books, 1982), p. 72.

6. Richard Hofstadter, *Social Darwinism in American Thought* (Boston: Beacon Press, 1944), pp. 31–50.

7. Ibid.

8. George Homans, *Social Behavior* (Boston: Harvard University Press, 1982).

9. Albert Einstein, *Ideas and Opinions* (New York: Bonanza Books, 1954), p. 153.

10. Constance Smith and Anne Freedman, *Voluntary Associations* (Boston: Harvard University Press, 1972).

11. Jane Addams, *Democracy and Social Ethics* (Cambridge, Mass.: Harvard University Press), p. 2.

12. Eleanor Roosevelt, "Mobilization for Human Needs," unpublished speech, Sept. 28, 1939.

13. Quoted in Sar Levitan, *The Great Society's Poor Law: A New Approach to Poverty* (Baltimore: Johns Hopkins Press, 1969), p. 3.

14. Frederick Jackson Turner, *The Frontier in American History* (New York: Henry Holt and Co., 1920), pp. 1–38.

15. Alexis de Tocqueville, *Democracy in America* (Garden City, N.Y.: Anchor Books, 1969), vol. 1, p. 53.

16. The extent to which American social policies have resulted in redistribution of income is discussed in Christopher Jencks, *Inequality: A Reassessment of the Effect of Family and Schooling in America* (New York: Basic Books, 1972); Winifred Bell and Robert Lekachman, *Public Policy and Income Distribution* (New York: New York University Press, 1974); Clair Wilcox, *Toward Social Welfare: An Analysis of Programs and Proposals Attacking Poverty, Insecurity and Inequality of Opportunity* (Homewood, Ill.: Richard D. Irwin, 1969).

17. Smith and Freedman, *Voluntary Associations*.

18. Ibid.

19. Robert Dahl, *Who Governs? Democracy and Power in America* (New Haven: Yale University Press, 1966).

20. Victoria Ortiz, *Sojourner Truth* (Philadelphia: J. B. Lippincott Co., 1974), p. 131. (Speech at Equal Rights Congress, New York City, May 9, 1867.)

21. Milton Friedman, *Capitalism and Freedom* (Chicago: University of Chicago Press, 1962).

22. Ibid.

23. Peter Steinfels, *Neo-Conservatives* (New York: Simon and Schuster, 1979).

CHAPTER THREE

How Technology Shapes Social Welfare

In the previous chapter we discussed values, one critical element in America's social welfare institution. Values, we saw, are the fundamental beliefs on which American attitudes toward social issues are based. They represent what we feel should be done, the oughts and ought nots of social welfare. They are often expressed in statements of philosophy, of goals and ends.

We come now to a quite different element of the social welfare institution: technology. Technology represents not what should be done about a given problem, but what *can* be done. It concerns propositions of fact; it offers a hypothesized relationship of cause and effect; it invites testing and verification. In sum, it deals with means, not ends. Taking an example from another field, let us consider the development of the atomic bomb during World War II. This was a triumph of technology, of understanding certain relationships of cause and effect and using that knowledge to produce a specific result. The decision to drop the bomb, however, was not a technological one. A formula could not be derived to prove whether or not America *should* use the bomb. That decision involved questions of value—of morals and ethics and philosophy—not technology.

VALUES AND HUMAN SERVICE TECHNOLOGY

The difference between what we should do and what we can do is an important one in the analysis of American social welfare. The previous chapter dealt with the first; the present chapter considers the second and its relationship to the first.

In the context of social welfare, we shall use the term "human service technology" to indicate the application of technology to social problems. Human service technology can be defined as follows: "the sum total of the knowledge, procedures, and techniques, that, when applied in a given human service field, will yield desired, predictable results."[1] This definition makes clear that human service technology involves *only* what can actually be done to alleviate a given social problem. Our values may lead us to agree as a society that it is right, for instance, to attack the problem of poverty or mental illness or drug abuse, but if the technology to do so is not available, or is not sufficiently developed, the programs that emerge from this value are unlikely to succeed. This is an important concept, because even in times when values favor social intervention, if we do not have the technological skill to achieve our agreed-upon goals, the resulting lack of progress may be detrimental to the social welfare institution. Social intervention will be perceived as ineffective, and the impact of failed programs will remain as a legacy. The level of technological development in the human services, then, becomes a crucial factor in the dynamics of social welfare.

The word "technology" summons images of computer components and space travel, of gleaming machinery and complicated mathematical formulas. While there are some common elements between this "high tech" and human services technology, there are also important differences. Because the goal of the human services is to effect a change in individuals or groups and because these changes are often intangible, the expertise involved is generally less precise than other technologies and more difficult to synthesize and assess. It is by no means impossible, however, to analyze human service technology; indeed, much can be learned from this effort, since it helps to clarify both the capacities and the limitations of the social welfare institution. In this chapter, therefore, we will discuss the two principal phases of human service technology, social problem analysis and social intervention. We will then conclude, as we did with values, by considering the implications of the points we have discussed for the social welfare institution.

Problem Definition and Values

Before any technology can be selected and applied, it is necessary to have a clear perception of the nature of the social problem being attacked. The importance of this step becomes apparent when questions such as the following are considered: Why does poverty exist? Why does mental illness exist? What causes unemployment? What are the factors leading to juvenile delinquency? Our answers to these questions depend to a significant extent on our values. Therefore, these questions are qualitatively different from, What steps lead to nuclear fission? That question is truly a technological one, the answer to which can be verified and tested; what works can be decisively distinguished from what does not work.

The questions related to social problems are far more controversial and involve such unscientific factors as ideology and passion. In science the technological and value elements are both present, but they tend to be more clearly separated, as in our example of the atomic bomb. In social welfare and human services, values are more entwined and far less readily distinguishable from technology. In social welfare, a policymaker or practitioner may readily and unwittingly confuse what is "correct" or "incorrect" with what he feels to be "right" or "wrong."

Since social welfare planning and implementation take place in the public domain, they are highly influenced by the values discussed in Chapter Two. If, for example, we know how to cure mental illness from a technological perspective, our solution may still only be accepted if it is consistent with prevalent values. A technological approach involving extensive intervention, for instance, will not be endorsed if traditional values such as self-reliance are widely held. Similarly, if technical analysis leads us to conclude that the mentally ill require lifelong support, the values of productivity and competition may prohibit that technologically derived approach from being applied.

Temporizing values also can provide a basis for resisting technical findings. Solid research data might well produce policy recommendations that would be impossible to implement because of concerns for compassion or equality of opportunity. Like most societies, Americans expect social decisions to reflect social values; few would argue for a value-free application of technology, even human service technology. We may value expertise, but at the same time we believe that it ought to be controlled. The precise degree to which we temper the use of human service technology with values is itself a question of value and will be considered in the later chapters of this book.

THE TASK OF SOCIAL PROBLEM ANALYSIS

Let us move from considering problem definition in relation to values to an examination of the overall process of social problem analysis. How much do we actually know about the causation and nature of social problems? This question must not be confused with what people maintain they know or with what we believe about social problems. Rather, what do we *actually* know? When we visit a doctor for a specific ailment, we are concerned with his ability to identify exactly what is wrong with us, not with what he believes is wrong with us, nor with what society feels about the ailment or about us. Technology can only be based on that which is actually known.

The question of what we actually know about social problems is a very difficult one, but it is obviously pivotal in examining the nature of social welfare, because it is the major factor which determines the potential success or failure of the programs that compose the institution of social welfare. We will not undertake here to introduce a system for categorizing everything we know and all we still need to know about the social problems that plague our society. We will set ourselves a more limited goal, to explore the nature of social problem analysis. What kind of analysis has informed the process of planning our social programs and deciding which technologies to apply?

Two Policy Premises: Human Development
and Societal Resource

Ways of approaching social problems can be categorized into two groups, or policy premises: Human Development and Societal Resource.[2] What distinguishes the two is the perceived location or origin of the social problem: where its root causes are thought to lie. The human development premise holds that the beginning point in the analysis of a particular social problem is the individual and his or her behavior.[3] The factors considered may be motivational, cultural, attitudinal, or genetic; they may involve such characteristics as skills, experiences, or perhaps physical attributes. The important point is that all these elements lie within the individual. The societal resource premise, on the other hand, focuses on the structures of society. It considers the distribution of income, the structure of political power, and the availability of jobs and education—in other words, the general accessibility of resources within a given social structure. Thus, the human development premise addresses its primary attention to the attributes and characteristics of individuals, whereas the societal resource premise looks at the structures and resources of the society surrounding the individuals.[4]

Social Stratification: Policy Premises at the Theoretical Level

In order to understand the theoretical distinctions between these two premises of social problem analysis, let us briefly consider a fundamental theoretical controversy from the field of sociology. This is the question, closely linked to our discussion in the last chapter: Why are some members of society more successful than others? Exploration of this question falls under the general area of social stratification theory. The controversies in this field will help illustrate the distinctions between the two premises we have been discussing.

The field of social stratification theory has a wide literature, but a few key articles suggest its basic arguments and are therefore most important for our purposes. The first, "Some Principles of Stratification" by Kingsley Davis and Wilbert E. Moore, begins by demonstrating that all societies have some system of stratification. None has achieved pure equality. Davis and Moore argue that inequality is functional for the maintenance of society. They reason that certain functions in a society are more important than others (for the maintenance of that society) and therefore require special skills and talents in order to be carried out effectively. Only a limited number of individuals possess the talent and ability to perform in the positions fulfilling these functions. Thus, the society is faced with an important task: "It must concern itself with motivation at two levels; to instill in the proper individuals the desire to fulfill certain positions, and once in these positions the desire to perform the duties attached to them."[5] The result of this task is the linking of societal rewards and reinforcements, such as superior status, prestige, and wealth, to these functional positions in order to attract talented individuals. "Social inequality is thus an unconsciously evolved device by which societies insure that the most important positions are conscientiously filled by the most qualified persons."[6]

Another view of social stratification is offered by Talcott Parsons. His conceptualization is based on the same primary assumptions as that of Davis and Moore. In considering the question of upward mobility, for example, in terms of the desire to attend college (a primary means of rising in the society's system of stratification), Parsons maintains that a heavy emphasis falls on the factor of motivation to mobility on the part of the boy himself and of his parents on his behalf as distinguished from objective opportunity for mobility. This is a conclusion which runs contrary to much "Liberal" opinion but is at least well enough validated by evidence to warrant further sociological investigation. . . .[7]

Essentially, we may state that within this framework, the focus is on the "free choice" of the individual. Therefore, his motivation to "get ahead" and the qualitative direction in which he wishes to do so, must be treated as qualities of his personality rather than placing the problem in the understanding of the exigencies of the structure in which he must act.[8]

Trimmed to its essentials, the argument that Davis and Moore are making is that some people have achieved a higher level in the society and have acquired more than others because they personally possess the characteristics required to fulfill certain select positions in the society. Parsons takes a similar line, arguing that the process by which one rises in the society is also based primarily on the "qualities of his personality." What is established, then, is a theory of social position based on individual characteristics.

Other studies and analyses that parallel this approach have focused, not on those who succeed, but on those who do not. Such studies have identified and documented a whole range of dysfunctional characteristics among those at the bottom of the social stratification ladder: low motivation, alienation, pathology, low incentive, authoritarianism, inability to defer gratification, dependence, inferiority feelings, illegitimacy, fatalism, weak ego, matriarchal family structure, social disorganization, deep-seated distortion, marital instability, inability to interact with community institutions, superficial interpersonal relationships, suspicion of people outside the family structure, poorly developed voluntary associations, low levels of participation, little interest in the rest of society, and dogmatism.[9]

A different view of social stratification is offered by Melvin Tumin, who argues that the societal search for individuals with talent to fill functionally important positions does not take place with "all things being equal" as he feels the Davis-Moore article implies. Such variables as class, race, religion, and sex play a far greater role in determining the structure of stratification than the mere possession of talent or skill. Tumin points out that stratification is a self-perpetuating phenomenon which, over time, prevents upward mobility by those at the lower levels despite their inherent potential.

Smoothly working and stable systems of stratification, wherever found, tend to build in obstacles to the further exploration of the range of available talent. This is especially true in those societies where the opportunity to discover talent in any one generation varies with the differential resources of the previous generation. Where, for example, access to education depends on the wealth of one's parents, and where wealth is differentially distributed, large segments of the population are likely to be deprived of the chance even to discover what are their talents.[10]

Whereas Davis and Moore see stratification as productive and functional for society, Tumin sees it as repressive and limiting: "Social stratification systems function to provide the elite with the political power necessary to procedure acceptance and dominance of an ideology which rationalizes the status quo, whatever it may be, as 'logical,' 'rational' and 'morally right.'" [11]

The central point for our discussion is not the intricacies of theoretical detail that these arguments offer, but their points of departure. Clearly, the Davis-Moore argument, like that of Parsons, provides support for the Human Development premise. The focus of the analysis is on individuals' personal characteristics as an explanation for their relative places in society. The theory, whatever its merits, suggests that further speculation and analysis would appropriately be focused on the individual strengths of those who prosper in a given society and the individual deficiencies of those who fail to rise. The Tumin argument leads in the opposite direction, lending support to a different premise; it encourages one to analyze the structure of society's resources and the nature of their distribution. The point of departure is different, and therefore the internal logic of the theory carries the analysis in a different direction.

Applying Policy Premises to Social Problems

In policy planning, as in theory building, problem analysis depends very much on one's choice of premise. Once that choice is made, the decisions that follow can safely be placed within the realm of objective analysis and can therefore be included in the domain of technology. On what basis, however, is the fundamental choice of analytical premise made? It is a difficult question, but certainly value and belief are critical influences.

Some social problems, such as alcoholism, for example, may seem by definition more appropriate for analysis from a Human Development perspective, yet there are aspects of Societal Resource involved as well, such as the need for additional programs or funding sources. Some might argue that a cause-and-effect relationship exists between the two approaches, that certain deficiencies in the structure of society, such as chronic unemployment and structural poverty, may lead to higher rates of alcoholism among the poor, whereas social norms, job-related tension, and inadequate alcohol counseling at the work place may increase alcoholism among the middle class.

Ideally, an approach based on either the Human Development or Societal Resource premise would also draw ideas and insights from the alternative premise. In the world of scholarship, the precise equation for blending the two approaches in addressing each social problem could offer ample opportunity for further speculation, discussion, and refinement. In the world of policy, however, where decision making, program construction, and implementation are pressing necessities, finely tuned distinctions are rapidly converted into broad program choices. The grays, through the necessity of action, become black and white, and the path not taken may in fact contain a large measure if not all of the truth. In the world of policy it is not the subtleties of analysis that are important but the fundamental premises that guide program development.

Let us look, for example, at the differences in premise in two books that were extremely influential in the 1960s. *The Negro Family: The Case for National Action* by Daniel P. Moynihan states:

> What then is the problem? We find that the answer is clear enough. Three centuries of injustice have brought about deep-seated structural distortions in the family life of the American Negro. At this point, the present tangle of pathology is capable of perpetuating itself without assistance from the white world. The cycle can be broken only if these distortions are set right. In a word, a national effort toward the problems of negro Americans must be directed toward the question of family structure. The object must be to strengthen the negro family so that it can rise and support its members as do other families. After that, how this group of Americans chooses to run its affairs, take advantage of its opportunities, or fail to do so, is none of the nation's business.[12]

A Human Development premise is illustrated in this quotation, which summarizes the basic Moynihan argument. The location of the problem, and hence the target of solution, is "the structural distortions" or the "tangle of pathology" of the "negro family." Something is clearly dysfunctional with the way in which this kind of family operates; it does not "rise and support its members as other families do." The author's recommendation is to "strengthen the family" and then let it take advantage of existing opportunities (presumed to be sufficient) with no further need for assistance or attention.

A quotation from an equally influential book, Harrington's *The Other America*, illustrates the Societal Resource premise:

> The real explanation of why the poor are where they are is that they made the mistake of being born to the wrong parents, in the wrong section of the country, in the wrong industry or in the wrong racial or ethnic group. Once that mistake has been made, they could have been paragons of will and morality, but most of them would never have had a chance to get out of the Other America.[13]

Harrington's view is that the structure of society is determinant. Once a person is born into certain groups or classes, his own resources can never be sufficient to alter his situation. Hence, for Harrington, individual group and family attributes and dysfunctions are not the locus of analysis; the answer lies instead in society's distribution of resources. Although both Moynihan and Harrington leave room to some extent for alternative explanations, their basic premises are clear and suggest significantly different directions for social policy.

Laid out in sequential steps, each premise's explanation of poverty follows logically, once its point of origin is accepted. From the perspective of the Human Development premise, poverty originates in the characteristics of the poor:

1. Those who are poor have unique traits; hence they are different. Their differences are significant and can be isolated.
2. The differences lie in patterns of behavior, cultural patterns, and the qualities of personality.
3. Such traits can be viewed as "deviant," "dysfunctional," and "pathological" in terms of the dominant cultural patterns of the rest of society.
4. Such traits constitute a mechanism for the perpetuation of poverty.[14]

The analysis of poverty from the perspective of the Societal Resource premise focuses on systems rather than individuals:

1. Poverty is essentially beyond the control of the poor.
2. The mechanisms for the perpetuation of poverty lie in the functioning of social systems.
3. Upward mobility is based on the degree of access to systems of opportunity and therefore is dependent on their flexibility and permeability.

Another social problem is mental retardation. From the human development perspective, the issue is primarily physiological:

1. Brain damage and other physical disabilities are the central problem in mental retardation.
2. Psychological factors are associated with or grow out of the physiological factors.
3. Mentally retarded persons' own inherent limitations severely restrict what can be done to address their problems.

Mental retardation, however, can also be viewed from a societal resource viewpoint:

1. There is a lack of adequate facilities and opportunities for the retarded.
2. Other social problems, such as poverty, can cause or aggravate mental retardation, by limiting adequate nutrition, prenatal care, infant health services, and early screening.
3. Public attitudes toward the mentally retarded can significantly affect their functioning and quality of life.

The problem of unemployment provides another example. The Human Development premise would offer the following argument:

1. The unemployed lack the motivation to find employment.
2. The unemployed lack the necessary attitudes and personal characteristics necessary to maintain a job.

3. The unemployed lack the necessary skills to fit the jobs that are available.
4. The unemployed are unwilling to accept the jobs that are available.

The Societal Resource approach to unemployment might suggest the following:

1. The job market does not provide sufficient jobs at adequate wages.
2. Access to employment is substantially blocked for some segments of society.
3. The educational system and other programs for training are inadequate and do not sufficiently prepare the labor force.
4. Information about employment opportunities is not made available in an organized way throughout society.

Other social problems such as crime, domestic violence, alcoholism, and drug abuse could be analyzed in a similar way, beginning with either premise and building from that starting point. It can be argued, of course, that elements of both premises are required for a complete and useful analysis. Ideally, a highly developed understanding of social conditions would include knowing precisely which analytical premise needs to be applied to which aspect of a given social problem and to exactly what degree each should be applied. A quantification of these factors would yield a system of multiple differentially weighted variables; the result would be a knowledge base on which a sophisticated human service technology might rest. No such technology exists at present; social policy choices tend to be closely associated with one analytical premise or the other, not so much because of their technical validity as because they are consistent with the values of those making the choice.

SOCIAL PROBLEM INTERVENTION

The Rehabilitative and Reconstructive Premises

When the Human Development premise guides social analysis, it leads most frequently to what can be termed the rehabilitative premise in the realm of policy. If the problem is located in the individual, then that is where the solution must lie as well. If the characteristics of the individual are dysfunctional in some way, then rehabilitation is required.

If, on the other hand, the Societal Resource premise shapes the original analysis of the problem, then some alteration in the structure of society is likely to be the policy outcome. Hence, rehabilitation and reconstruction become the fundamental policy alternatives, and the selection of technology follows logically from the choice of premise. Changing the jobless is a rehabilitative policy; changing the labor market is reconstructive. From a technological perspective, programs that train and educate individuals, for example, the Job Corps, are rehabilitative. Programs that create jobs, for example, the New Deal's WPA, are reconstructive.[15]

Many programs, of course, reflect a combination of the two policy alternatives. This occurs, for instance, when different program elements have been added at different times, under the influence of different policy premises. Consider public welfare, for example. This program as originally established under the Social Security Act of 1935 was reconstructive in concept, in that it redistributed money from the general tax revenues to the poor, thus altering how American society allocated its resources. The growing influence of the Human Development premise in the 1960s, however, led to the addition of a service component, clearly aimed at the rehabilitation of public welfare recipients. Social services provided under this amendment are intended to alter the clients' dysfunctional characteristics, including their approaches to family life, parental roles, marital relationships, social and civic relationships, economic skills (such as budgeting) and household skills (maintenance of the home, upkeep of furnishings, and so forth).[16] Clair Wilcox summarizes the historical relationship in public welfare between what we have termed the rehabilitative and reconstructive alternatives:

> As originally envisaged, it was the purpose of public assistance to assure a minimum of subsistence for adults who were in need and to provide for the care of dependent children. This was done by giving them small amounts of cash. The program was frankly a palliative, not one through which the causes of poverty were to be attacked. In time, however, it came to be argued that the program's emphasis should be shifted from relief to rehabilitation; that its beneficiaries should be made self-supporting; that dependency should be lessened and the need for assistance payments reduced. This approach would give more help in the form of services and less in the form of cash. It was the approach of the social worker who viewed poverty as a matter of maladjustment that was to be corrected through the methods of casework. The view that emphasis should be shifted to rehabilitation was endorsed by Congress in 1962 in a series of amendments to the public assistance law. The enactment was hailed by social workers as a landmark in welfare history. But its influence on the character of the assistance has not, as yet, been great.[17]

Housing programs for the poor are another example of how both rehabilitative and reconstructive approaches may be applied to the same social issue:

> Obviously, those who are poor require improved housing conditions. The question is: how is this to be done? One approach is to construct new housing facilities and make them available to the poor through some kind of public housing program. This, of course, is a hard service which attempts to remedy the lack of societal resources in the area of housing. Another approach, the Rehabilitative, is to concentrate efforts on slum dwellers in attempting to help them cope with existing conditions by helping them to improve their homemaking and housekeeping skills, etc. In the former case, a tangible item is being transferred, in the latter a skill or attitude is the target of service.[18]

Unemployment insurance, also established under the Social Security Act of 1935, provides one more example of rehabilitative and reconstructive approaches coexisting within a single program. In this case, different levels of government appear to have been guided by different policy premises. As set up by the federal government, unemployment insurance was primarily reconstructive, designed simply as an income transfer program. In administering the program, however, many states have added requirements that those who receive funds must furnish proof that they are seeking employment, under threat of being terminated from the program. Regulations such as this add a rehabilitative element to unemployment insurance, since they suggest the presence of dysfunctional motivation and behavior in the recipient. Presumably, the threat of being cut off from funding will motivate some recipients to seek work who might otherwise have continued on unemployment insurance.

Human Service Technologies:
Reconstructive and Rehabilitative

Analytical premises (Human Development and Societal Resource) lead to policy premises (rehabilitative or reconstructive). These in turn determine the kinds of technologies that will be used to address social problems.

Rehabilitative technologies generally involve the provision of intangible services (not money or food or housing) personally provided by specially trained staff to a recipient who is expected to benefit from the interaction. For instance, counseling, one of the most frequently used rehabilitative technologies, is offered in specialized forms to the aging, the young, alcoholics, drug abusers, the mentally ill, the mentally retarded, rape victims, child abusers, ex-convicts, the bereaved, couples, and families. The goal of counseling is usually to stabilize or improve the client's emotions or behavior; again, the focus is less on the conditions that disturb the client and more on the client's ability to cope emotionally with these conditions.

Other rehabilitative technologies focus on other aspects of the client that have presented either the individual or society with difficulty: the client's health, motor skills, intelligence, vocational level, behavior. A large number of professionals are involved, including physicians, social workers, nurses, psychologists, teachers, occupational therapists, recreational therapists, child-care workers, alcoholism counselors, drug counselors, youth workers, and employment counselors.

The model used by all these professionals is basically one of casework, involving a personal application of expertise to an individual client so as to improve his or her condition or abilities. The technologies of casework are varied and difficult to assess; they draw on various bodies of knowledge from a number of fields of scholarship. Psychoanalytic theory and ego psychiatry, for instance, provide a theoretical base for psychotherapy, but they also have had broader influence throughout the field of counseling. Behaviorist theory has contributed as well; its influence can be recognized well beyond the specific area of behavior modification to which it was originally applied. The field of social work has contributed several models of casework. Other models have emerged from occupational therapy, recreational therapy, vocational rehabilitation, medicine, and nursing. The goal of all these technologies is to improve individual functioning, either in a general way or in specific problem areas.

Reconstructive programs focus on rearranging systems rather than on changing clients. The provision of financial benefits through public assistance, for instance, is fundamentally reconstructive, since it involves the redistribution of funds from higher-income taxpayers to low-income recipients. Even Social Security and unemployment insurance, while drawing on recipients' own previous contributions, play a reconstructive role, since they restructure recipients' income so that they pay into the system when they are in a position to do so and receive its benefits when their ability to earn is reduced. Programs that provide in-kind benefits, such as food or housing, are also reconstructive, involving as they do the reallocation of finite, consumable resources to those who could not have bought them with their own funds.

The technologies associated with reconstructive efforts are much less clearly defined than those in the rehabilitative area. Indeed, some human service professionals trained in the rehabilitative tradition—as most are—have questioned whether the more impersonal, system-oriented work of reconstruction is an appropriate use of their skills and abilities. To some extent, these doubts are justified. Once established, a program offering financial assistance or in-kind benefits clearly requires less intensive professional involvement on a daily basis than a program of counseling or physical rehabilitation.

Even rehabilitative programs may evolve through a reconstructive process. Thus, to offer prevocational training for the mentally retarded is rehabilitative. To identify the inadequacy of existing prevocational opportunities, to design and lobby for a new program, and to change admission policies so that mentally retarded clients with emotional problems can also be served—these activities, all drawing on a knowledge and understanding of human service technology, are reconstructive.

VALUES, TECHNOLOGY, AND THE SHAPE OF SOCIAL WELFARE

In analyzing social welfare, it is apparent that what we know about social problems is closely intertwined with what we believe about them. The basic policy premise, then, rehabilitative or reconstructive, may be chosen not on the basis of technical decision making, but to a great degree on the basis of values. This is the case because the choice between analytical premises precedes the policy choice and involves a process outside the realm of scientific methodology or empirical verification. As noted in the beginning of this chapter, in order to analyze the social welfare institution it is vital that we recognize the different roles played by values and technology. It seems apparent that analytical premises (and the policy premises that flow from them) are often selected on grounds other than strict adherence to technological consideration. In short, the things that we know how to do in the human services may only be drawn upon if they are consistent with more fundamental decisions about analytical approach and policy direction.

It is clear that these decisions are influenced by social values through a process quite different from considerations of their effectiveness when actually implemented. As noted, a highly developed technology might tell us, in its analytical aspects, precisely where each premise was appropriate and to what extent. From this, theoretically, would follow the policy alternative and its appropriate program application. Yet values would still limit the application of such a technology, even if it were available. The powerful influence of these values on technological decisions is a given in the consideration of social welfare. The resulting impact on social programs will be considered in Part II.

In considering the characteristics of human service technology, then, one difference between the process of putting a man on the moon and constructing social policy is clear. In the former case, once the decision to undertake the task is agreed upon, technology predominates, providing the most effective means toward achieving this goal. Program and beliefs do not dictate trajectories nor the use of fuel. In the application of human service technology, on the other hand, the ability to make value-free judgments about the effectiveness of different technical choices is much more limited. As we analyze the social welfare institution at any given period, then, it is appropriate to ask three questions:

1. Does the human service technology in use reflect a predominantly rehabilitative or reconstructive approach to social problems?
2. Does the choice of one approach or the other reflect an objective analysis of the problems involved?
3. Will that choice contribute significantly to solving the problems identified?

As was the case with value clusters and their conflicting positions on social intervention, technology, too, represents a choice between two different analyses and policy approaches. Our choice of one or the other may in fact be the result of a process that is neither consistent nor rational from the perspective of policy outcome, yet the effects of that choice on the shape of social welfare are enormous. Our discussion suggests that it is unrealistic to expect that technological choices can—or perhaps should—be made on a value-free basis. It is critical, however, that we remain aware of the part that values play in such choices. Their impact is reflected, not only in how technological approaches are designed, but also in the area we will be discussing next, the structure of social welfare.

SUMMARY

This chapter began with a discussion of the difference between values, which suggest what *should* be done, and technology, which shows what *can* be done. It is values, we suggested, that set the parameters within which technology operates. Social problems are first defined and conceptualized in terms of values.

Technology involves two principal stages, social problem analysis and social intervention. In the first, problems are generally approached from one of two perspectives: the Human Development premise or the Societal Resource premise. The former focuses on the characteristics of the individual that may have initiated or aggravated the social problem being addressed. The latter places primary emphasis on social systems and structures that may contribute to the problem.

From the analysis of the problem comes the plan for its solution. From the Human Development premise comes a policy premise that focuses on rehabilitation of the client; from the Societal Resource premise comes a different premise, advocating changes in social systems. Various examples were given in which the same problem, considered from different angles, could be explained and addressed in terms of one premise or the other.

Each policy premise is associated with particular types of human service technology. The rehabilitative premise gives rise to technologies focused on changing or improving the client: for example, teaching, counseling, and psychotherapy. The reconstructive premise involves technologies that initiate and manage social change, including needs assessment, public education, program planning, and administration.

Human service technology, it is clear, is closely linked to social values. Whether or not this relationship is ideal, it is essential to recognize it and understand its implications for social welfare.

NOTES

1. Charles Perrow, "The Analysis of Goals in Complex Organizations," *American Sociological Review* 26 (6), 1961, pp. 854–866.

2. This choice represents the most basic point of departure in the formulation of social policy. It is fundamentally a choice of value. The decision about technology or the means must follow.

3. Again, the choice of premise is intrinsically a value choice.

4. Clearly the choice of policy premise is a highly political one. Although the record is mixed, the liberal tendency is in the direction of societal resource and the conservative, human development.

5. Kingsley Davis and Wilbert Moore, "Some Principles of Stratification," *American Sociological Review* (10), 1945, p. 246.

6. Ibid., p. 243.

7. Talcott Parsons, "A Revised Analytical Approach to the Theory of Social Stratification," in *Class, Power and Status*, ed. Reinhard Bendix and Seymour Lipset (Glencoe, Ill.: Free Press, 1953).

8. Ibid.

9. Oscar Lewis, "The Culture of Poverty," in *On Understanding Poverty: Perspectives in the Social Sciences*, ed. Daniel P. Moynihan (New York: Basic Books, 1970), pp. 191–192.

10. Melvin Tumin, "Some Principles of Stratification: A Critical Analysis," *American Sociological Review* 10 (4), 1953, p. 380.

11. Ibid.

12. Daniel P. Moynihan, *The Negro Family: The Case for National Action* (Washington, D.C.: U.S. Government Printing Office, 1965), p. 47.

13. Michael Harrington, *The Other America: Poverty in the United States* (New York: Macmillan Company, 1962).

14. Such a view was the basis of the culture of poverty thesis that greatly influenced the Great Society programs of the 1960s.

15. Many of these examples can be found in the services provided by the Charity Organization Societies of the late nineteenth century.

16. Clair Wilcox, *Toward Social Welfare* (Homewood, Ill.: Richard Irwin, 1969), p. 339.

17. Ibid., p. 311.

18. Robert Pinker, *The Idea of Welfare* (London: Heinemann Books, 1978), p. 38.

CHAPTER FOUR

The Structure of the Social Welfare Institution

In the previous two chapters we discussed two of the social welfare institution's principal elements: values and technology. Now we add the third element: structure. In the analysis of a social institution it is necessary to look not only at the belief system that drives the institution and the technical assumptions under which it operates, but also at how the institution is organized to perform its work. An institution's structure is its organizational form, the system of relationships among its component parts that determine the flow of power and resources. In the analysis of structure, questions like these arise: What are the relative roles between levels of government? How does funding flow? Who determines priorities? Who sets standards? What interactions are necessary to set a program in motion? How do public and private sectors relate to each other? How much autonomy does any single component of the institution have?

The American social welfare institution is tremendously complicated, with interrelationships among all the various levels of government—federal, state, county, and municipal—as well as with the vast and diverse private sector. No brief analysis can begin to capture every detail of this intricate structure. Yet it is essential that we try to understand its most significant characteristics, since in doing so we will begin to understand more about the social welfare institution itself.

In previous chapters we showed that both values and technology can be discussed in terms of continua. As the balance between temporizing and traditional values alters, for instance, there is an associated tendency toward either intervention or nonintervention in social problems. Similarly, in technology there is a range of choices between policy premises that emphasize rehabilitation and those that stress reconstruction. Now, in the analysis of structure, the critical characteristic we will examine will be the tendency toward centralization or decentralization. Many of the most important historical changes in the structure of social welfare, we will show, can be conceptualized as movement in one direction or the other along this continuum; the centralization/decentralization dimension is helpful, too, in understanding social welfare structure as it stands today.

We will begin by exploring the meaning of centralization and decentralization in the social welfare institution: What are their characteristics, and how do they each enhance or obstruct the ability of the social welfare institution to achieve its goals? To further this discussion, we will then examine the subject of centralization and decentralization in terms of those instances in the past in which the organizational structure of social welfare underwent significant change.

CENTRALIZATION AND DECENTRALIZATION

When an institution is wholly centralized, all its efforts are centrally controlled and administered. Resources feed into a central point and are allocated from there, all priorities are centrally determined, and the degree of autonomy diminishes dramatically as one moves toward the outer edges of the institution. It would be hard to find an example of total centralization among American institutions, but those that tend in this direction are characterized by a high level of coordination, close control of resources, and a single set of shared priorities.

Many observers have noted the usefulness of centralization at the federal level, where it is important to maintain national consistency. Sometimes this consistency is simply a question of uniform technical standards; it would be impractical, for instance, for different states to have different emission standards for cars or significantly different food and drug laws. Sometimes consistency is a matter of equity. There is an obvious advantage to having the same Social Security benefits nationwide, and some observers have recommended a similar approach for other programs, like Aid to Families of Dependent Children (AFDC).[1] Sometimes consistency is required by the issue involved; Eizenstat and Kahn cite air pollution as an example of the kind of problem that cannot be dealt with adequately by the laws of any single city or county because its ramifications are broader than any one community's jurisdiction.[2]

Centralization is a particularly effective structure when there is a need for combined efforts toward common goals. Wartime, for instance, generally involves increased centralization; indeed, it is no accident that political leaders seeking to centralize efforts toward social welfare goals often use wartime imagery. Franklin Roosevelt's first Inaugural Address spoke of the need "to move as a trained and loyal army willing to sacrifice for the good of a common discipline," "a unity of duty hitherto evoked only in time of armed strife," and his own duty to lead "this great army of our people, dedicated to a disciplined attack upon our common problems."[3] Similarly, Lyndon Johnson chose to announce his plan for a centralized federally directed economic opportunity program with these words: "This administration today, here and now, declares unconditional war on poverty."[4] The power of the federal government to invite or compel collaboration toward national goals—what Reichley calls "the federal cutting-edge"[5]—is a critical feature of centralization in the structure of social welfare.

One national goal for which centralization at the federal level has been particularly important is that of responding to the needs of the poor and of ethnic and racial minority groups. The national government has often been seen as more responsive than states and localities to the vulnerable members of society,[6] and action to enhance the lives of these groups and protect their rights has tended to come at the federal level. National legislation like the Civil Rights Act of 1964 and the Voting Rights Act of 1965, has reinforced the perception of the central government as a vigorous advocate for the underprivileged. At the economic level, the federal government has played the principal role over the past fifty years in creating and funding *redistributive* programs, those which shift benefits, by means of transfer payments or services, from higher to lower income groups. In general, as Dommel points out, a move toward federal centralization has meant an increase in such programs, while a move to decentralize policymaking to the states has tended to produce nonredistributive programs that benefit all citizens equally. "The major advances that have been made by . . . disadvantaged groups over the past forty years," he says, "have come about by elevating decision making to the national level."[7]

These, then, are the principal strengths of centralization in social welfare: the rationality and equity of nationally consistent standards, the coordinative power of national leadership, and the tradition of commitment to the needs of the disadvantaged.

At the other end of the continuum lies decentralization, characterized by a tendency to disperse policymaking rather than to coordinate it. In a sense, a totally decentralized institution is no longer an institution, since in its movement along the scale it has lost all the characteristics that held it together—shared resources, mutual goals, interdependent elements. There are, however, a considerable number of institutions that lean strongly in the direction of decentralization. In these cases one is likely to see considerably more autonomy in the various elements that make up the whole, priorities may be set separately, resources may be obtained and allocated independently, and there may be less emphasis on coordinating the work of the different components.

One of the advantages of such an approach is the greater freedom it permits at the state and local levels to develop programs suited to local conditions. Social circumstances vary from area to area, and some degree of decentralization is necessary to ensure that externally developed solutions are not imposed where they do not apply. Miringoff and Carvalho liken the appeals of decentralization to those of grass-roots politics: "local control, participation, firsthand knowledge of local conditions, and freedom from dictation by the central government."[8] Eizenstat and Kahn cite the issue of access for the handicapped as a case where overly ambitious regulations were developed centrally; they suggest that state and local levels, with their more practical understanding of the difficulties involved in implementation, could have produced more workable guidelines if the policymaking had been done in a more decentralized way.[9]

Decentralization is not only helpful in protecting lower units of government from unreasonable standards. It can foster experimentation as well, since it leaves individual localities freer to try out approaches that may not be sufficiently proven to justify national application. As the centralized programs of the New Deal grew from experimentation at the state level, as elements of the War on Poverty could trace their roots to programs tested by various cities and private foundations, so some degree of decentralization is helpful to encourage the exploration of ideas and approaches that may later be replicated nationally through centralized structures.

The proliferation of social welfare programs in the 1960s, each with its own requirements, target groups, and application procedures, provided another argument in favor of decentralization.[10] Rather than tie the localities' hands with separate standards, application procedures, and reporting requirements for hundreds of special-purpose grants, it was argued, federal funds should be provided with fewer strings attached. The revenue sharing initiated by President Nixon in 1972 and the block grants begun under President Reagan in 1981 represented steps in this direction. Now the principles of decentralization were to be applied, not only to program design but to priority setting as well. Again, decentralization was an appealing model because of its ability to encourage creativity, ensure the local applicability of social welfare policies, and protect communities from the arbitrary or unreasonable requirements that excessive centralization was felt to have produced in the past.

It should be clear from the above discussion that both centralization and decentralization in social welfare have much to recommend them. Centralization has proved to be an effective structure for coordinating and inspiring national efforts; but it has also sometimes led, as its critics point out, to overly specific standard setting, leaving little room for local variation. Decentralization, on the other hand, can at its best provide greater latitude for innovation and local problem solving and can reduce some of the more burdensome aspects of bureaucratic record keeping. At its worst, it has sometimes created a climate in which state and local officials pursued a path of rather narrow local self-interest without sufficient regard for the needs of either the wider society or for the less privileged groups within their own communities. The answer, though it is not easily achieved, is to develop a social welfare structure that represents some effective balance between the two ends of the continuum, one that will both protect local individuality and meet the wider needs of society and its most vulnerable members.

PERIODS OF STRUCTURAL CHANGE

To explore further the issue of centralization and decentralization, let us examine some examples of significant structural change in the past, starting with the pre-Progressive era.

Pre-Progressive Era: A History of Decentralization

In the years before 1900, American social welfare was highly decentralized, based almost entirely on private initiative at the local level. Two traditions were most evident during the nineteenth century—individual philanthropy and small-scale community-based associations. Interestingly, it was the association that came first. In the early days of the nineteenth century, before the great fortunes of the post-Civil War years emerged, the most common way of meeting social need was the informal pooling of efforts among friends and neighbors. Visiting in 1835, Alexis de Tocqueville commented:

> Americans of all ages, all stations in life, and all types of disposition are forever forming associations. . . . Americans combine to give fetes, found seminaries, build churches, distribute books, and send missionaries to the antipodes. Hospitals, prisons and schools take shape that way. . . . In every case, at the head of any new undertaking, where in France you would find the government or in England some territorial magnate, in the United States you are sure to find an Association.[11]

As the century progressed, the amount of charitable activity intensified, but the decentralized character of social welfare remained relatively unchanged. By 1878 there were 800 voluntary charitable agencies in Philadelphia alone, compared to just 33 fifty years earlier.[12] Even where national associations began to emerge—such as the new Charity Organization Society (ancestor of the Community Chest) and American branches of the Salvation Army, YMCA, and Red Cross—they did not at first represent a significant difference in social welfare structure, since individual chapters were still usually organized, funded, and administered almost entirely at the local level.

The second approach to social welfare, individual philanthropy, represented, of course, an even more decentralized structure. Charitable contributions by the rich took on particular significance in the second half of the nineteenth century as the concentration of wealth was facilitated by the nation's growing industrialization, the building of the railroads, and the *laissez-faire* economic policies of the national government. Andrew Carnegie, in his article entitled "Wealth," offered the principle of "stewardship," which somehow made every personal fortune a part of the divine plan. "Thus is the problem of Rich and Poor to be solved," he wrote:

> The law of accumulation will be left free; the laws of distribution free. Individualism will continue, but the millionaire will be but a trustee of the poor; entrusted for a season with a great part of the increased wealth of the community, but administering it for the community far better than it could or would have done for itself.[13]

Under Carnegie's doctrine, the provision of social welfare might be seen to reach the outer limits of decentralization, with each successful capitalist working entirely on his own to assess social needs, determine solutions, and provide the necessary funds. In 1889 it did seem possible that "stewardship" represented the coming trend in American social welfare, in which even the small-scale coordination of local associations would be replaced by an entirely decentralized system of individual philanthropy.

But another event took place in 1889 that suggested a different path for the social welfare institution. In a poor neighborhood in Chicago, the most famous American settlement house, Hull House, opened its doors. By 1891 there were six settlement houses in the United States; by 1910 there were more than 400.[14] These settlement houses were in one sense continuing the tradition of local associations. But in another sense they represented something new in social welfare because of their focus on entire neighborhoods rather than specific social problems or client groups. In their communities they became hubs of activity, crossing every kind of organizational barrier—social, ethnic, political, religious—in an effort to bring opportunity and well-being to those they served. No problem was too esoteric or specialized for the settlement houses to address. Clinics and day nurseries were established, followed by playgrounds, clubs, libraries, boarding homes, bathhouses, and even cooperatives for buying coal.

By the end of the nineteenth century, the structure of American social welfare, while still highly decentralized, was beginning to show the first signs of a tendency toward more coordination. National associations, though still loosely structured, continued to emerge, and in their own communities the settlement houses demonstrated on a small scale the value of attacking a wide variety of social problems through a single centralized effort.

It will be noted that at no point in this discussion of social welfare in the pre-Progressive Era has state or federal action been mentioned. In fact, during the nineteenth century social welfare was almost universally seen as a local and primarily private issue. The attitude of these years is conveyed by Grover Cleveland's words, when he was urged to distribute seed to drought-stricken farmers: "I do not believe that the power and duty of the general government ought to be extended to the relief of individual suffering."[15] Thus, when we speak of the 1890s as reflecting the first beginnings of a movement toward centralization, we are not speaking of centralization under state or federal direction as it emerged in later years, but simply of more coordination at the local level, especially in the private sector. In the terms used in Chapter One, it was forces outside government—individuals, reformers, and voluntary organizations—not those inside that took the first steps toward centralization in the years before 1900.

Progressive Era: State Government
Enters the Field of Social Welfare

During the Progressive Era (1900–1918), social welfare moved toward greater centralization with the emergence of state governments as increasingly active partners in the social welfare institution. To a great extent, this change evolved from reformers' practical experience with the limitations of private intervention in solving social problems. Jane Addams of Hull House, for example, began her settlement house work with a vision of direct, purely personal service to those in need. "There is to be no 'organization' and no 'institution' about it," wrote her friend Ellen Starr. "The world is overstocked with institutions and organizations; and after all, a personality is the only thing that ever touches anybody." [16] Over time, however, the settlement house workers began to see that no amount of individual dedication could resolve problems like polluted water, dangerous working conditions, lack of medical care, irregular garbage collections, and systematic poverty. Only through governmental effort could the overwhelming social difficulties of the new immigrants, the victims of industrialization, and the mass of urban poor be comprehensively addressed. As this realization grew, not only among settlement house workers but among all those who wished to see social conditions improved, it began to seem more and more crucial to convince the American people that social welfare was a matter of public policy.

In the years between 1900 and 1918, the combined efforts of liberal politicians, writers, teachers, clergymen, social workers, feminists, ethnic leaders, and a host of others were focused on moving social welfare onto the public agenda. They were convinced, one participant recalled, that "if the people only knew the facts, they would act to remedy the situation." [17] Richard Hofstadter notes the significance of this effort:

> So far as those important intangibles of political tone were concerned in which so many Progressives were deeply interested, they won a significant victory, for they heightened the level of human sympathy in the American political and economic system. . . . In a large and striking measure the Progressive agitations turned the human sympathies of the people downward rather than upward in the social scale.[18]

Gradually the reformers' advocacy began to bear fruit in social legislation at the state level. Step by step, issue by issue, the individual states began to take responsibility for social programs that heretofore had either not existed or had been provided on a voluntary basis, the quality and scope depending on the inclinations of individual citizens in each community. Slowly the pendulum began to move in the direction of centralization.

Wisconsin pioneered the way, led by "Battling Bob" La Follette, who was elected governor in 1900. There the nation's first state-level industrial commission was created to oversee the health and safety of working conditions. A workmen's compensation law was introduced, child labor significantly reduced, a minimum wage law for women instituted, and appropriations for the state university tripled. More than a hundred other laws were passed designed to improve social, economic, and political conditions in the state. So powerful was the appeal of La Follette's program of centralized social reform under government leadership that the movement continued unabated when he left the governorship for a Senate seat in 1906.[19] Twenty years later, Wisconsin was still in the forefront of national reform.

But if Wisconsin was a pioneer, the rest of the country was close behind. By 1910, New York, California, New Jersey, Michigan, Iowa, North Carolina, and Texas had initiated significant programs of Progressive reform,[20] and nearly every state could point to new pieces of Progressive social legislation. Gradually, the private decentralized structure of social welfare was giving way to a new pattern in which state governments provided centralized resources and leadership for the effort to improve social conditions. The order in which issues were addressed varied, and each state program developed differently. But the theme of state government as an active and centralizing force in the structure of social welfare was common throughout.

In 1907, Massachusetts created the first Commission on Old Age Pensions, Annuities and Insurance to coordinate county programs; over the next decade a majority of other states began to take a larger role in problems of the elderly. The first state workmen's compensation law was passed in New York in 1911; five years later, more than thirty states had followed suit. Illinois and Missouri led the way on widows' pensions, followed gradually by nearly every state in the union. Other kinds of social legislation emerged as well—on industrial safety, public health, care of the disabled, and a host of other issues—each one reinforcing the concept that ensuring social welfare is a legitimate activity of government.

Where the reformers of the Progressive Era did not achieve their goals, they prepared the ground for later action. In 1913 the first American conference on social insurance was held, drawing attention to the progress already made in Europe. Year in and year out, the reforming effort went on: bills were proposed, books written, speeches made, new bills proposed. When, in 1923, Montana became the first state to pass a law for statewide old-age benefits that held up in court, it represented the culmination of lobbying, planning, and public education in dozens of legislatures since the turn of the century. Efforts like these succeeded, in Montana and elsewhere, not because centralization had an intrinsic appeal to those who supported it, but because it seemed the only practical way to address problems whose scope and gravity were too great for smaller-scale efforts. During this period, the circumstances described in Chapter One as preconditions for social reform—social problems widely recognized, feasible solutions proposed, articulate and collaborative outsiders, sympathetic insiders—combined to create an atmosphere in which significant changes in the structure of social welfare were possible.

The fact that, by the beginning of the New Deal, most states offered workmen's compensation, twenty-nine paid old-age benefits, and forty-five paid widows' pensions, that twenty-five state legislatures had at least debated state unemployment insurance and that, overall, the responsibility of state government for assuring individual welfare was generally recognized—all these accomplishments were directly attributable to the efforts during the Progressive Era to move the American social welfare institution toward greater centralization under government auspices.

The New Deal: Centralization Moves to the Federal Level

The next major change in the structure of social welfare took place during the New Deal (1933–1940), and again it was in the direction of centralization. Now the leadership was not state government but federal, justified by the terrible urgency of the Depression. Rapid and sweeping intervention seemed essential in order to avoid national calamity; only the federal government, it was clear, had the power and resources to do what was needed.

If the period of the New Deal had followed immediately after the Progressive Era it might have seemed like the logical next step in the gradual process of centralizing social welfare under governmental auspices. But in fact more than a decade intervened between the two periods, during which the move toward a more centralized structure was slowed and in some places reversed. Individual states continued, one by one, to adopt pieces of social legislation, but far fewer new initiatives were launched. Inside and outside government, the drive for reform lost power; the country, it seemed, was gradually drifting back toward the more decentralized social welfare structure of the nineteenth century.

Only the shock of the Depression, in which bank failures, factory closings, and mass deprivation left state governments as paralyzed as their people, set the stage for another surge toward centralization, this time under federal direction. By the time of Franklin Roosevelt's inauguration, the gross national product had fallen from $80 billion to $40 billion, wage income had dropped 60 percent, 9 million savings accounts had been lost, and 15 million people were out of work. In such an atmosphere, Herbert Hoover's reverence for the ''principles of decentralized self-government, ordered liberty, equal opportunity and freedom to the individual''[21] seemed insufficient. People wanted help, and they were prepared to support almost any system that could deliver it.

The challenge to the American social welfare institution in 1933, which had passed by default to the federal government, was twofold: to provide immediate assistance to those in need and to devise more permanent economic security programs for the long term. Immediate relief came first, organized principally through the Federal Emergency Relief Administration (FERA). While the Hoover Administration had loaned money at 3-percent interest to the states for relief activities during the previous summer, FERA provided direct grants on a scale far beyond any previous undertaking; Congress approved half a billion dollars in its first appropriation.

Speaking of FERA later, Roosevelt wrote: "From the very beginning two important points were evident: (1) The operations of the program, aside from certain basic standards and stipulations, were to be decentralized and local in character, and (2) work, rather than idleness on a dole, was preferred."[22] Both points were debatable. The provision of emergency relief was in fact considerably more centralized than Roosevelt was ready to admit, and federal relief played at least as large a part in sustaining people over the next few years as the New Deal's employment programs. That Roosevelt would speak in this way may be a measure of his ambivalence, and of that which he sensed in the American people, toward the changes his administration had set in motion. But ambivalence or no, the structure of American social welfare was being transformed.

Under the Emergency Recovery Act that created FERA, states or localities were only supposed to receive one dollar for each three they had expended on relief in the previous quarter; this formula, however, was soon found to be insufficient. Federal help was needed, whatever the community's past expenditures had been; increasingly, assistance from Washington was seen as a major source of support, not simply an augmentation of local programs. This growing reliance on federal funding was one important departure from previous approaches to social welfare. The second followed from it: Because of Washington's central role in the provision of emergency relief, the ERA administrator, Harry Hopkins, was able to impose certain national program standards. He insisted, for instance, that relief recipients be given cash, not vouchers, for groceries, and he extended relief payments for the first time to cover the cost of clothing, shelter, and medical care, as well as food.[23] The federal government's new role in the structure of social welfare, based initially on its unique ability to raise and distribute funds, thus moved quickly to include a broader kind of centralization encompassing standards and priority setting.

The New Deal's employment programs developed along similar lines. First came the Civilian Conservation Corps (CCC). Because this program was designed to serve a particularly difficult group of the unemployed who had few community ties—the rootless young men who frequented the nation's highways and urban slums—federal intervention seemed particularly appropriate. Soon thereafter came the Public Works Administration (PWA). Again, the idea of putting the unemployed directly on the federal payroll was somewhat controversial, but the focus of the program on large-scale public works that only the federal government was then in a position to fund and administer (bridges, tunnels, aircraft carriers, train stations, ports, sewage plants, courthouses, schools, and hospitals)[24] helped justify the expanding federal role. Each succeeding program—the Civil Works Administration which helped the country through the bitter winter of 1933–34 and the massive

Works Progress Administration established in 1935—further expanded the dimensions of the federal role.[25]

Again, federal funding created the opportunity for federal policymaking. Seeking to reinforce recipients' sense of dignity in its employment programs as it had in its relief efforts, the New Deal administrators designed innovative new work projects that provided opportunity for the exercise of a wide variety of skills. In addition to public construction, employment in their own fields was provided for white-collar workers, artists, writers, actors, teachers, historians, and a host of others.

Centralized administration of emergency relief and employment programs was accepted because it was generally agreed that no other private or public agency could amass and allocate enough resources fast enough to meet the national crisis. States participated actively, of course, in the effort—as did a multitude of private agencies and municipalities—but it was clear to people across a broad range of political opinion that a centralized effort under federal direction was essential. By 1940 the ERA, PWA, CWA, and WPA had all been phased out; what remained was the new assumption that in time of social or economic crisis the federal government was the central and most crucial actor in the structure of social welfare.

If the New Deal had created only its emergency programs for relief and employment, the face of American social welfare would have been changed profoundly. But during the same period it undertook an even more ambitious kind of reform, the creation of programs that would help ensure future economic security. New agencies were created to support and stabilize a whole range of areas in which the federal government had previously taken little action: the Home Owners' Loan Corporation, Tennessee Valley Authority, National Recovery Administration, Federal Housing Administration, U.S. Housing Authority, Rural Electrification Administration, Farm Security Administration, and National Labor Relations Bureau. Other acts expanded the power of existing federal departments to regulate the nation's social and economic life: the Agricultural Adjustment Act, the Fair Labor Standards Act, and the Public Contracts Act. Each new bill expanded further the central role of the federal government. But perhaps no legislation had so profound an effect on the structure of social welfare as the Social Security Act of 1935.

In the years after World War I, many states had instituted partial social security programs, but few were comprehensive. Many benefited only parts of the population because of their reliance on voluntary participation by counties or municipalities, and some programs, such as unemployment insurance, had made almost no headway. It seemed clear that it would be a very long time before the states, working separately, developed a comprehensive nationwide system of social insurance. Federal initiative seemed the answer.

In August 1935 the Social Security Act was passed. It contained ten titles, four of which had to do with establishing a compulsory contributory system of federally administered old-age retirement benefits. The remaining six titles covered grants to the states for assistance to the indigent elderly, unemployment insurance, aid to dependent children, maternal and child welfare, public health services, and assistance to the blind.[26]

The sections of the Social Security Act creating the federal old-age retirement plan represented the most clear-cut departure from previous structures. For the first time, a network of federal offices, staffed by federal employees, would administer a social program that would deal regularly, year in, year out, with millions of Americans. Social welfare was again being centralized, but this time the action was not being justified on the basis of short-term emergency need; the Social Security Administration was to become a permanent and major part of the American social welfare institution.

Although the six remaining titles of the Social Security Act worked through grants to the states, they too differed significantly from state-initiated welfare programs of earlier years. With these titles, the federal government asserted its concern for a whole range of social problems—unemployment, the indigent elderly, dependent children, maternal and child health, public health services, and the blind—and made available money that it could in turn withhold if states did not participate according to federal expectations. In every title except that of public health (which was under direct control of the U.S. Public Health Service), there was a requirement for the submission of a state plan, which had to receive federal approval before grants could be made. Thus, even in the parts of the Social Security Act not directly administered by the federal government, there was an opportunity for federal review, standard setting, and prioritization. The federal government was now a principal actor in the resolution of social problems. The American social welfare institution had taken another significant stride along the continuum toward centralization.

The Great Society: Centralization and Decentralization Coexist

The next period of significant change in social welfare, the Great Society, created a new phenomenon: a social welfare structure that was highly centralized in terms of leadership, standards, and funding, yet was extremely decentralized at the program level, almost approaching the structural characteristics of social welfare during the early years of the century. Let us review some of the circumstances that led to this development.

The years between 1940, when the New Deal gave way to preparations for World War II, and 1963, when President Johnson took office, brought relatively little change to the structure of social welfare. The war years, while tending to reinforce the strong central role of the federal government, were not a period in which domestic issues commanded much interest. In the period that followed, as in the 1920s, the issues of social welfare remained at the level of discussion and debate, but few substantive changes took place. The expansion of the federal role into national health insurance, for instance, was proposed by Truman but defeated in Congress, then taken up by congressional liberals under Eisenhower, and later proposed unsuccessfully by President Kennedy in the early 1960s.[27] Similar efforts, also unsuccessful, were undertaken in the areas of civil rights and federal aid to education. In the terms outlined in Chapter One, this postwar period saw a slowly growing national consciousness of social welfare issues, the development of preliminary proposals for addressing the problems identified, and a gradually expanding coalition of "outsiders" and "insiders" pressing for structural change. This period, in short, helped create the climate for the Great Society but brought little actual change in the social welfare institution.

With the assassination of President Kennedy in 1963, conditions changed dramatically. The national shock over Kennedy's death, the growing awareness of poverty, the dramatic appeal of the civil rights movement, and President Johnson's own political leadership combined to create a new consensus for social reform. Structural change in the social welfare institution followed rapidly.

The first great effort, and in some ways the most striking of all the Great Society's social legislation, was the Economic Opportunity Act of 1964. At one point in the early discussions of the bill, Johnson had suggested that federal responsibility for the program might be limited to nine months, after which state and local governments could take it over.[28] But by the time of the State of the Union address in January 1964, the project had become a highly centralized national crusade—a War on Poverty. "It will not be a short or easy struggle—no single weapon or strategy will suffice," said Johnson, "but we shall not rest until that war is won."[29]

The Economic Opportunity Act of 1964, through which the War on Poverty was to be waged, contained seven titles and established funding for the following program areas:

1. Youth employment (established Job Corps, a work-training program that became the Neighborhood Youth Corps, and work-study grants to students)
2. Community action
3. Loans to farmers and new programs for migrant workers
4. Loans to small businesses
5. A domestic version of the Peace Corps (VISTA)
6. A clearinghouse to support voluntary contributions to needy children
7. Basic education for adults

The centralizing aspects of the Economic Opportunity Act are most easily recognized. Like earlier reformers in the Progressive and New Deal eras, the planners of the War on Poverty envisioned a growing arena for governmental intervention in the area of social welfare. Creating an environment in which the federal government acted sometimes as actual service provider, more often as catalyst and funding source, the Economic Opportunity Act placed the federal government ever more firmly in the center of the nation's social welfare efforts. "It is the policy of the United States to eliminate the paradox of poverty in the midst of plenty in this Nation," read the Preamble;[30] the language of the act made clear that this effort would be shaped, guided, and funded by the federal government.

The evidence of the centralizing aspects of the Economic Opportunity Act is so compelling that the simultaneous beginnings of a trend toward decentralization are sometimes overlooked. But they are there, below the surface, and they provide powerful early indications of the structural changes that evolved more decisively in the 1970s and 1980s.

Most clearly in Title II, which established the Community Action Program, but implicit throughout the act is the willingness of the federal government to bypass established structures, particularly state and local governments, in order to create the programs needed.

> Title IA empowers the Director of the Office of Economic Opportunity to create Job Corps centers through agreements with "any Federal, State or local agency or private organization;"[31]
>
> Title IB describes the work-training programs as being provided through grants to "state and local agencies and private non-profit organizations" and specifies that, while coordination with existing programs is desirable, "where such services are inadequate or unavailable, the program makes provision for the enlargement, improvement, development and coordination of such services. . . ."[32]
>
> Title IC authorizes the OEO Director to arrange work-study programs directly with institutions of higher education;[33]
>
> Title IIIA involves the provision of federal loans directly to low-income farming families;[34]
>
> Title IIIB allows for federal assistance to migrant programs offered by "states, political subdivisions of states, public and nonprofit agencies, institutions, organizations, farm associations or individuals;"[35]
>
> Title IV establishes federal loans directly to owners of small businesses;[36]

Thus in each program area, Washington reserved the right to reach past the traditional intervening political layers—state, county, and municipal governments—and deal directly with individual organizations, institutions, and families.

Underlying this profound structural change was a growing doubt that traditional structures—most notably state and municipal governments—were sufficiently responsive to the needs of the poor. One of the reasons the Economic Opportunity Act was needed, it was felt by some, was that state programs to address poverty had been half-hearted or ineffective. Numerous examples seemed to bear this argument out—the disinterest of state employment programs in the hard-core unemployed, the treatment of migrant workers by the states and counties through which they passed, the historical indifference of rural-dominated state legislatures to urban problems, and the resistance of some city governments to the needs of their own poor and minority citizens. Now was the time, under federal leadership, to establish direct links between the federal government and those who needed help.

No section of the Economic Opportunity Act exemplified this thinking so clearly as Title II, which created the Community Action Program. Title II provided federal funds to almost any nonprofit group, public or private, that developed programs "of sufficient scope and size toward the elimination of poverty," so long as the programs were "developed, conducted and administered with the maximum feasible participation of residents of the areas and members of the groups served."[37]

Patrick Moynihan, then in the Department of Labor, recalls that at the time "no one in authority at either end of Pennsylvania Avenue regarded the participation clause as noteworthy."[38] It had appeared in the first draft of the legislation and remained untouched in the final bill Johnson signed, without apparently arousing either comment or concern. Yet the requirement for "maximum feasible participation" of the poor turned out to be a storm center of political controversy as neighborhood groups all across the country seized upon its possibilities in their struggles with state and local governments, as well as with other established institutions. In these struggles, the federal government, as represented by the Office of Economic Opportunity, became an ally of the neighborhood groups against intervening levels of government. Whatever the moral and political effects in terms of empowering the poor, the structural result was in the direction of decentralization. Ever since the turn of the century, programs of social welfare had been moving toward tighter coordination and more central administration. Now, although federal funds were essential to the effort, the trend in terms of administrative control had made a giant leap from Washington, over the state houses and the city halls, to the level of neighborhood associations and block clubs.

If the Economic Opportunity Act had been a single example of this dual trend toward and away from centralization, it would still be noteworthy because of the important historical role it played. But the contradictory structural themes that characterized it were repeated in much of the legislation that followed. Centralization, in terms of enhanced federal involvement and influence, was reinforced with each bill. Some, such as Medicare, Medicaid, the Elementary and Secondary Education Act, Head Start, and Neighborhood Legal Services, represented federal entry into areas where it had never ventured before. Other bills simply provided new funds for existing programs, making federal support an increasingly important part of the social welfare structure. By 1970 federal funds represented 83 percent of all expenditures on social insurance, 58 percent of expenditures of funds for public aid, 48 percent of those for health and medical programs, 12 percent for education, and 83 percent for housing.[39]

But the important central role played by the federal government in initiating and pushing through new programs was offset to a considerable extent by the decentralizing effect of dealing directly with thousands of small organizations, neighborhoods, and interest groups. In the past such programs had been channeled through state and local governments, which had provided coordinative structures at each level; now, because of the feeling in Washington that such structures had inhibited the responsiveness of social welfare efforts in the past, a direct link was established between the federal government and an enormous range of beneficiaries. Now nearly every community had multiple power centers in the field of social welfare, often operating with little coordination and sometimes in cutthroat competition. Organized by race, age, profession, philosophy, gender, or neighborhood, these groups played an increasingly powerful role in national policymaking, since the new legislation put the federal government in direct communication with all of them.

The Elementary and Secondary Education Act, for instance, involved direct grants to individual school districts; Medicare created a partnership between the federal government and the nation's wide variety of health-care providers; Model Cities created new community development organizations in hundreds of cities, often working in direct opposition to municipal planning agencies; and Legal Services empowered federally appointed lawyers to help local residents in suits against local institutions. Even the Voting Rights Act brought federal appointees to advocate and intervene for individual voters against their local election officials. Each bill served to reinforce the patterns established by the Economic Opportunity Act: consolidation of the federal leadership role in social welfare (centralization), balanced by a climate of increasing autonomy and activism among recipient groups (decentralization).

Given this structure, the federal government by the very centrality of its role became a focal point for the disillusion that followed as soon as the programs to eliminate poverty proved unequal to the promises. As federal commitment and resources waned, the atomization of social institutions was more and more evident. Richard Nixon's 1968 presidential campaign slogan captured both the mood of the country and the people's wish that it were otherwise: "Bring us together again."

In spite of this slogan, over the next ten years the Nixon, Ford, and Carter administrations gradually resolved the inherent contradictions in the Great Society's dual approach to social welfare structure by moving in the direction of decentralization. Federal expenditures on social programs were generally maintained, but the federal role in administering the funds was increasingly relinquished to the states. Officially, the new expanded state and local programs continued to function under federal guidelines. But after 1968 the heart of social welfare administration moved from Washington to state capitols and to county and municipal government. This trend, which underlies today's social welfare institution, is explored in the next chapter.

SUMMARY

We began this chapter with a discussion of the continuum—centralization to decentralization—through which changes in the structure of the American social welfare institution can be analyzed. We then traced the history of these changes, starting with the decentralized, primarily voluntary structures of early nineteenth-century America. As social problems became more profound and more visible, we saw the movement toward a greater centralization of social efforts, first at the state level during the Progressive Era and then at the federal level during the New Deal. Then, after a period of contraction and consolidation, came the Great Society with its unusual duality—centralization through the role of federal government as the driving force in social welfare and decentralization through the dispersion of influence and initiative to a multiplicity of groups and organizations. Finally, in the years since 1968, we have seen a gradual abandonment of the centralizing federal role, replaced by the delegation of increasing responsibility to state and local governments.

NOTES

1. See, for example, Advisory Council on Public Welfare, *Having the Power, We Have the Duty* (Washington, D.C.: U.S. Government Printing Office, 1966); President's Commission on Income Maintenance Programs, *Poverty amid Plenty: The American Paradox* (Washington, D.C.: U.S. Government Printing Office, 1969); Henry Aaron, *Why Is Welfare So Hard to Reform: A Staff Paper* (Washington, D.C.: Brookings Institution, 1973); Jerry S. Turem, "Can We Fix AFDC?" *Public Welfare* 40 (4), Fall 1982, pp. 24–29. For accounts of President Nixon's effort to create a standardized federal system, see Martin Anderson, *Welfare: The Political Economy of Welfare Reform in the United States* (Stanford, Calif.: Hoover Institution, 1978); Daniel P. Moynihan, *The Politics of a Guaranteed Income: The Nixon Administration and the Family Assistance Plan* (New York: Random House, 1973); Rowland Evans, Jr. and Robert D. Novak, *Nixon in the White House: The Frustration of Power* (New York: Random House, 1971). For an account of President Carter's effort toward standardized public assistance, see Joseph A. Califano, Jr., *Governing America: An Insider's Report from the White House and the Cabinet* (New York: Simon and Schuster, 1981).

2. Stuart E. Eizenstat and Paul W. Kahn, "A Rational Federalism," *Public Welfare* 41 (2), Spring 1983, p. 18.

3. Samuel Rosenman, ed., *The Public Papers and Addresses of Franklin D. Roosevelt* (New York: Random House, 1938), vol. 2, pp. 11–15.

4. Lyndon B. Johnson, State of the Union Address, Jan. 8, 1964, *Public Papers of the Presidents of the United States: Lyndon B. Johnson, 1963–1964* (Washington, D.C.: U.S. Government Printing Office, 1965), book 1, p. 114.

5. A. James Reichley, *Conservatives in an Age of Change: The Nixon and Ford Administrations* (Washington, D.C.: Brookings Institution, 1981), p. 158.

6. See, for example, E. E. Schattschneider, *The Semi-Sovereign People* (New York: Holt,

Rinehart and Winston, 1960); Eizenstat and Kahn, "A Rational Federalism," p. 21; J. L. Pressman, *Federal Programs and City Politics* (Berkeley: University of California Press, 1975); Richard Cole, "Revenue Sharing: Citizen Participation and Social Services Aspects," in David Caputo, ed., *General Revenue Sharing and Federalism* (Philadelphia: American Academy of Political Science, 1975), pp. 63-74.

7. Paul R. Dommel, *The Politics of Revenue-Sharing* (Bloomington, Ind.: Indiana University Press, 1974), p. 35.

8. Lee M. Miringoff and Barbara L. Carvalho, "Reagan's Bloc Grant Decentralization Policy: A Framework for Analyzing the Current Transition in Local Programs," *Journal of Applied Social Sciences* 8 (2), Spring-Summer 1984, p. 232.

9. Eizenstat and Kahn, "A Rational Federalism," p. 21.

10. See, for example, Will S. Myers, "A Legislative History of Revenue Sharing," in Caputo, *General Revenue Sharing*, p. 3; Paul R. Dommel and Associates, *Decentralizing Urban Policy: Case Studies in Community Development* (Washington, D.C.: Brookings Institution, 1982), p. 14; Sara A. Rosenberry, "National Social Welfare Commitments under the Reagan Administration," *Journal of Urban Affairs* 5 (1), Winter 1983, pp. 1-15; Beryl A. Radin, "Leave it to the States," *Public Welfare* 40 (3), Summer 1982, pp. 17-18.

11. Alexis de Tocqueville, *Democracy in America* (New York: Anchor Books, 1969), vol. 2, part 2, p. 513.

12. Carl Bakal, *Charity USA* (New York: New York Times Books, 1979), p. 26.

13. Andrew Carnegie, "Wealth," *North American Review*, June 1889, vol. 391, p. 663.

14. George Martin, *Madame Secretary: Frances Perkins* (Boston: Houghton Mifflin, 1976), p. 59.

15. Quoted in Charles I. Schottland, "Government Economic Programs and Family Life," *Journal of Marriage and the Family* 29 (1), February 1967, p. 74.

16. Quoted in Anne Firor Scott, introduction to Jane Addams, *Democracy and Social Ethics* (Cambridge: Harvard University Press, 1964), p. xxiii.

17. Quoted in Archie Hanlan, "From Social Reform to Social Security: The Separation of ADC and Child Welfare," *Child Welfare* 45 (11), p. 495.

18. Richard Hofstadter, *The Age of Reform: From Bryan to F.D.R.* (New York: Vintage Books, 1955), pp. 243-244.

19. William L. O'Neill, *The Progressive Years: America Comes of Age* (New York: Harper & Row, 1975), p. 65.

20. Eric F. Goldman, *Rendezvous with Destiny: A History of Modern American Reform* (New York: Vintage Books, 1955), rev. ed., p. 132.

21. Herbert Hoover, *The New Day: Campaign Speeches of Herbert Hoover* (Stanford, Calif.: Stanford University Press, 1929), p. 168.

22. Quoted in Robert E. Sherwood, *Roosevelt and Hopkins: An Intimate History* (New York: Harper & Brothers, 1948), p. 44.

23. Ibid., p. 47.

24. William E. Leuchtenberg, *Franklin D. Roosevelt and the New Deal: 1932-1940* (New York: Harper & Row, 1963), pp. 133-134.

25. Arthur M. Schlesinger, Jr., *The Age of Roosevelt: The Coming of the New Deal* (Boston: Houghton Mifflin, 1958), pp. 263-281.

26. Social Security Act, Aug. 14, 1935, *United States Statutes at Large*, vol. XIX, pp. 62ff.

27. James L. Sundquist, *Politics and Policy: The Eisenhower, Kennedy and Johnson Years* (Washington, D.C.: Brookings Institution, 1968). See also Eric F. Goldman, *The Crucial Decade—And After: America, 1945-1960* (New York: Vintage Books, 1960).

28. Rowland Evans and Robert Novak, *Lyndon B. Johnson: The Exercise of Power* (New York: New American Library, 1966), p. 427.

29. Lyndon B. Johnson, *Public Papers of the Presidents*, book I, p. 114.

30. Economic Opportunity Act of 1964, *United States Statutes at Large*, vol. LXXVIII, sec. 2, p. 508.

31. Ibid., sec. 103(a), p. 508.

32. Ibid., sec. 113, p. 512.

33. Ibid., secs. 121-124, pp. 513-515.

34. Ibid., sec. 302, p. 524.

35. Ibid., sec. 311, p. 525.

36. Ibid., sec. 401, p. 526.

37. Ibid., sec. 201, p. 516.

38. Daniel P. Moynihan, *Maximum Feasible Misunderstanding: Community Action in the War on Poverty* (New York: Free Press, 1970), p. 91.

39. "Social Welfare Expenditures, Fiscal Year 1980," *Social Security Bulletin* 46 (8), August 1983, p. 16.

CHAPTER FIVE

Interactive Forces in the American Social Welfare Institution

In Part I, three elements of the American social welfare institution—values, technology, and structure—were introduced, and the range of approaches to social welfare within each element was explored in terms of a continuum:

1. In the area of values, discussion focused on the level of commitment to social intervention, which tends to be less when traditional values (such as individualism and efficiency) are in the ascendant and greater when such views are softened by temporizing values (such as compassion and service).
2. In the area of technology, the policy premises that were explored ranged from those stressing rehabilitation of the client, at one end of the scale, to those stressing reconstruction of social systems, at the other.
3. In the area of structure, the focal issue was degree of centralization. Discussion covered a range of structures along this continuum, from systems where power and resources are highly dispersed to those in which both are under unified central control.

The discussion of each of these elements separately in Part I has laid the groundwork for Part II, in which we will explore the interaction among the three—that is, the dynamics of social welfare—and apply them to current policy and program. We will begin this chapter with an overview of how values, technology, and structure interrelate, and then proceed to an analysis of the general dynamics at work in the social welfare institution today. The following two chapters will carry this analysis further: Chapter Six will apply these dynamics, expressed in operating principles, to the program level, and Chapter Seven will explore the impact of these principles on the individuals most involved—the clients and staff of the social welfare institution. By the end of Part II, it is hoped, a broad picture of today's social welfare institution will be established, setting the stage for a discussion in Part III of possible directions for the future.

VALUES, TECHNOLOGY, AND STRUCTURE: A CIRCULAR RELATIONSHIP

The Impact of Values

Values, technology, and structure form a circular relationship. Each influences the other to form an overall dynamic by which we can better understand social welfare. Let us begin our discussion of this dynamic by considering the impact of values. Values determine how social well-being is defined; they also establish the political and psychological environment within which the social welfare institution operates. In most cases, decisions about the technology and structure of social welfare are strongly influenced by values—often more strongly than the decision makers realize. "It is now apparent," wrote Milton Friedman a number of years ago, "that disagreement about values often masquerades as disputes about facts.''[1] Because people's beliefs are so integral to their way of seeing the world, they often overlook the influence of their values on what they conceive to be a purely rational process of decision making.

In the area of social welfare technology, for instance, it is the general preference to picture a process in which objective skills are weighed, selected, and applied to social problems in a nonjudgmental and value-free way. But whatever the objective knowledge base may be, each technical intervention is filtered through the values of the intervener and of the society that surrounds him. Some of these values are part of each person's own cultural and family background; others are absorbed in the course of education and community life. Such values may be humanizing or constricting, temporizing or traditional, but they will inevitably influence the way in which the purely technical skills of social welfare are practiced. Services to single mothers, for instance, may be significantly different depending on the feelings that staff and the larger society hold about marriage, child care, and female roles. In the area of employment, reconstructive approaches, such as programs that create new jobs, will not be used at a time when values suggest that the chief reason for unemployment is lack of effort on the part of the worker. Nor will rehabilitative services, such as vocational counseling, predominate if the value system is emphasizing nondiscrimination and structural change in the labor market. Thus, values make a society—and the staff who implement social welfare policy—more or less responsive to certain kinds of technologies, quite apart from their logical appropriateness.[2]

The interplay of values and structure is, of course, similar. In a purely rational world, structure might simply represent the most logical way of organizing the services that technology dictates. But in different eras there are value-based preferences for greater or lesser centralization of services, growing from the national sense of urgency about the need for social intervention, the value being placed at that time on free choice and individualism, and prevalent feelings about the role of government. A magnificently conceptualized national health insurance system, for instance, will be irrelevant to a society bent on reducing the level of government involvement in daily life; similarly, a nutrition program that allows maximum participation for thousands of grass-roots organizations may miss the mark if the predominant national concern is rapid large-scale intervention.

The Impact of Technology and Structure

Both technology and structure, then, are profoundly influenced by values. Simultaneously they help create the environment in which values are formed. Values may spring from one's personal background, but they constantly interact with the events of everyday life. In the analysis of social welfare, technology and structure can be as significant in the shaping of values as the influences of philosophy, religion, or ethics.

Free choice, for instance, is an American value. Yet in the field of education, the relative success of the public education system and the fiscal realities of its administration have combined to limit the appeal of policies that would widen free choice, such as tuition tax credits or vouchers usable in private as well as public schools. In this case, then, practical experience with a given structure and technology have led Americans to place less emphasis on their value-based commitment to free choice.

Another example is the American system of veterans' services. In the midst of a society that has long resisted national health insurance and has shown a strong preference for the provision of health services through private rather than public auspices, the Veterans' Administration stands as a striking exception. "As an almost self-contained health system," Morris observes, "the VA directly maintains and administers over a hundred hospitals with some 100,000 beds, as well as a network of outpatient medical clinics, nursing homes and social services."[3] As in the case of public education, this specialized national health service has become an accepted part of the American social welfare institution; the relative success of its existing structure and technology have overshadowed the value-based considerations that might argue for its dissolution.

In summary, then, neither values, technology, nor structure necessarily holds the single dominant role in determining the course of social welfare. Each plays upon the other in a process that is continually changing and evolving. As a major illustration of this dynamic, let us consider the case of Medicare, the nation's system of health coverage for the elderly. Initiated in 1965 in the remarkable spring of the Great Society, Medicare has survived twenty years of changing politics and philosophies. Reviewing its development provides a clear illustration of how values, technology, and structure work together to shape social programs.

Values, Technology, and Structure:
The Example of Medicare

In the passage of Medicare, we see first the influence of values supporting social intervention in the enthusiasm for ensuring access to improved health care. Unusually for the United States, the Medicare program did not even include a means test; it was to serve all Americans over the age of sixty-five. Of course, the fact that only the elderly were eligible ensured that much of the program benefit would go to poor people, given the prevalence of poverty among that age group. Nevertheless, passage of Medicare represented a victory for interventionist values.

Technology played a part as well, offering a scientific answer to the problems of the elderly. On the whole, Medicare represented a reconstructive approach to health care; while the actual medical services it provided were not significantly different from those offered before, Medicare undertook to change profoundly the accessibility and financial availability of these services. For the first time, America's elderly (of whatever income level) could visit the doctor or hospital of their choice and use public dollars to pay for the services they received. This use of public funds to purchase medical care in the private sector was a significant innovation in the technology of American health care delivery.

When it came to structure, Medicare represented a significant departure from previous arrangements, but it is difficult to identify the movement as being toward or away from centralization, because it contained elements of both. At the administrative level, the change was decisively in the direction of centralization; although the elderly had been receiving retirement benefits for nearly thirty years under Social Security, the addition of universal health benefits under this federal system represented a marked increase in the degree of centralization. Yet at the same time we can see how values like free choice and private enterprise made their own contribution to the program, leading to the creation of a fundamentally decentralized structure. Under Medicare, hospitals were free to charge for "all reasonable costs," physicians were free to provide any services they felt necessary, and clients were free to use any physician and any hospital that would take them.

Gradually the chosen structure began to exert its own effect on technology: The very availability of funds for increasingly sophisticated medical services encouraged their use and then their refinement. Reimbursement structures offered no incentive for limiting the elaboration of technology, and values supported the expansion, emphasizing the right of all clients, rich or poor, to the very best in health care. The long-time American love affair with technology encouraged the trend, placing more and more emphasis on high-tech procedures and complicated machinery.

Then came a new phase: The value-based preference for opportunity and free choice began to collide with a more pragmatic concern over the geometric progression of health-care costs. Data began to suggest that much of the increased cost came from more expensive and elaborate services, rather than from a real increase in either the number of patients served or the general health of the population at risk. This led in the early 1980s to the adoption by the Department of Health and Human Services of a set of Diagnosis-Related Groups (DRGs), which were to form the new basis for Medicare reimbursement of hospital costs. Under this system, which began implementation in late 1983, hospitals would be reimbursed not for each day and each special service a patient received (as in the past), but for exactly the number of days of care that a patient with that diagnosis might, according to the DRG charts, be expected to need. If the patient stayed longer or ran up additional costs during his stay, the hospital would simply have to absorb the expense.

With this change in structure came a new technological challenge; if hospitals were to break even, physicians would have to be more discriminating in their use of hospital stays and medical services. The task now was not to provide the patient with every service he might conceivably benefit from, but to provide exactly the care—no more, no less—necessary for his recovery. Technical skill would now be addressed not only to seeing that every one of a patient's needs was identified, but to making sure that the patient received no unnecessary services.

At the same time that this reorientation was taking place within the health-care industry, lawmakers and health planners were exploring the advisability of still further changes. Each proposal carried still more implications for values, technology, and structure. Should Medicare benefits be limited to the poor? Should Medicare recipients be required to use only designated hospitals or physicians? Should health maintenance organizations be formed for Medicare patients, encouraging the use of outpatient services in preference to hospital care?

Meanwhile, other elements of the health system began to join in the ferment:

1. Between 1980 and 1983, Maryland, Massachusetts, New Jersey, and New York initiated new kinds of reimbursement structures affecting not only Medicare but also Medicaid, Blue Cross, commercial insurers, and self payers.[4]

2. In the same years, membership in health maintenance organizations across the country grew 50 percent, reaching 12 million by 1983.[5]

3. In Iowa, California, and Kansas, Blue Cross began experimenting with various cost-control plans.[6]

4. Five large companies—AT&T, Ford, Chrysler, WR Grace, and Citibank—opened discussions on having workers pay a larger share of their health expenses.[7]

5. Blue Cross/Blue Shield initiated an educational program for physicians in 1984 to reduce the incidence of unnecessary X-ray and similar diagnostic procedures.[8]

6. In its 1984 annual convention, the American Medical Association devoted special attention to voluntary limitation of fees as a way of avoiding more rigorous external controls.[9]

7. Ten New York City hospitals launched an experimental program in which a sampling of surgical patients would accept shorter than usual hospitalization or outpatient surgery.[10]

The ongoing debate on the costs of health care has focused, at least on the surface, on issues of structure: How is reimbursement to be managed? Who will pay the costs? What costs will be accepted? But interwoven in this discussion are profound questions of value and technology. So Medicare—a program that began primarily with a value-based response to human need and an awareness that technological skill was available to provide the desired services—led to the creation of a structure involving millions of dollars and touching millions of lives. Technology supported the growth of the structure; the structure supported the growth of the technology. A reassessment of values along more cost-conscious lines then led to a structural change (the introduction of the DRGs), which in turn reshaped the technological environment. Now, as the implications of these changes become more apparent, new issues of value, technology, and structure are being explored. And so the interplay continues, with each of the three elements shaping and being shaped by the other two.

We have chosen the example of Medicare to illustrate the interrelationship of values, technology, and structure. Other examples could have been chosen, where the various interactions occurred in different combinations or in different orders, but the fundamental elements would have been the same: values, technology, and structure, acting upon each other to shape the social welfare institution.

DOMINANT PATTERNS IN THE INTERACTION OF VALUES, TECHNOLOGY, AND STRUCTURE

Within each of the three elements of the social welfare institution we have chosen to analyze—values, technology, and structure—we have identified a continuum of approaches to social welfare, and we have shown how tendencies toward one end or the other of each scale are expressed in social policies. Of course, a system as complex as the American social welfare institution rarely represents a total commitment to one end of a scale or the other; at any point in time one can expect to find a scattering along the continuum, from values that encourage social intervention to those that minimize it, from rehabilitative to reconstructive technologies, from decentralized to centralized structures. In the example of Medicare, just reviewed, for instance, we noted the influence of values working both to expand intervention and to limit it, and we observed that the structure contained elements of both centralization and decentralization.

This diversity, however, is most noticeable when we examine individual programs. When one considers a whole era's approach to social welfare, more general patterns emerge. Then it is frequently possible to identify predominant tendencies toward one direction or the other within each of the three elements in our analysis. Thus, in a given period, it is usual to see one cluster of values (either encouraging or limiting social intervention) exerting more influence than the other, to notice that technologies generally lean more toward the rehabilitative or more toward the reconstructive, and to identify movement toward centralization or away from it.

These trends do not happen randomly. Given what we know about the interaction of the various aspects of the social welfare institution, it is not surprising to find that there are certain "tilts" in value, structure, and technology, which tend to occur together. Values that deemphasize social intervention, for instance, tend to stress individual responsibility for social problems, whereas those that encourage intervention generally involve a greater willingness to address other factors as well—environment, lack of opportunity, dysfunctional systems. It follows logically, then, that traditional values, to the extent that they favor any social programs, will lead most naturally to rehabilitative approaches, whereas interventive values are more likely to be associated with reconstructive approaches.

The kinds of values and technologies that predominate will also influence structure. Reconstructive technologies frequently lend themselves to more centralized approaches, since consistency and integration become more important when systems-level changes are sought. When rehabilitative efforts are being pursued, on the other hand, the need for centralization is much less evident. Here, the focus on the individual client's problems tends to encourage a case-by-case approach, diminishing the concern for coordination across programs. The traditional values frequently associated with rehabilitative approaches place a strong emphasis on localized responsibility and free choice, both of which are felt to be better served by a decentralized structure.

The example of the New Deal provides an illustration of these associated trends in social welfare. During the Depression, the traditional values of the twenties—individualism, self-sufficiency, and free choice—were displaced by a surge of support for social intervention. By 1933, it was far less necessary than in the Progressive Era for activists outside the government or sympathetic officeholders to bring social welfare problems to public attention; this time the evidence was all around. Under these circumstances, only a minority still insisted that individual rehabilitation was the answer to social problems; reconstructive change on a sweeping scale became the order of the day. For the immediate problems of poverty and unemployment, recipients were provided with money and jobs, not training and education. For the longer-lasting task of ensuring economic security, the New Deal developed a wide range of new programs, nearly all focused on changing systems, not clients. Price supports for farmers, insured mortgages for homeowners, pensions for the elderly, public housing for the poor, industrial codes for business, collective bargaining for workers—each program in its way attacked poverty and economic insecurity, but through reconstructive rather than rehabilitative technologies.

We observed earlier that the combination of interventionist values and reconstructive technologies is likely to be associated with centralized structures.

The example of the New Deal is an illustration of this tendency. While the financial devastation of the states and cities during the Depression undoubtedly gave extra impetus to the centralization of social welfare efforts at the federal level, such a structure might well have emerged in any case, given the scope of the changes being undertaken. As we noted in Chapter Four, centralization tends to facilitate unified large-scale efforts. The New Deal represented just such an effort. Shared values calling for expanded social intervention led to predominantly reconstructive technologies, which in turn encouraged centralized structures.

When, in the next section of this chapter, we look at our own time, we will see this principle of association in another context: values that tend to minimize intervention, leading to primarily rehabilitative technologies, carried out through increasingly decentralized structures. This current pattern, like that of the New Deal, will further illustrate our argument that trends in the social welfare institution move in relation to each other, with certain combinations occurring in associated patterns.

WHERE DO WE STAND?

Over the past decade trends in social welfare have tended to move in the opposite direction from the period of the New Deal: away from intervention, away from reconstruction, away from centralization. Instead, as traditional values have gained influence, there has been an associated tendency toward rehabilitative technologies and decentralized structures. This has been reflected in an emphasis on individual responsibility rather than collective intervention, the preference for case-specific approaches, the diminished integrative role played by the federal government. All these have encouraged an approach to social problems in which each client or each group of clients is treated in isolation. As a result, the social welfare institution has become increasingly fragmented.

From politics we have inherited the term "balkanization," which grew out of the internal wars of the Balkan states in Eastern Europe. Though together these small countries formed a considerable land mass, they expended their energies and wealth for years in struggles amongst each other. Although they shared common bonds, they chose to focus on what divided them and so poisoned relations with each other that they could never cooperate to resist their more serious enemies to the east and west.

The patterns that have begun to emerge in recent years represent a kind of balkanization of the American social welfare institution. Although the institution as a whole is rich in resources, its energies seem dissipated by particularism and fragmentation. Let us review the trends that contribute to this condition. Then, once we have an overview of the social welfare institution today, we will proceed in the next two chapters to discuss the practical impact of these trends on programs and on the individuals involved.

The Tilt in Values: A Reluctance to Intervene

Let us look first at the predominant values of today as they relate to social welfare. On the whole, do they lean toward or away from social intervention? Increasingly of late, it seems, a reluctance to intervene has guided social welfare policy.

During the Carter administration, Hamilton Jordan, the president's adviser, argued against new social policy initiatives. "The mood of the government is passive and nonpartisan," he told the president. "Americans want better government, not more government. That is why Carter was elected. The people do not want more programs."[11] Six years later, in a message to Congress, President Reagan reviewed what his administration had accomplished as they had sought to act on the mandate Jordan perceived:

> I worked with the Congress to reverse the growth of Government programs that had become too large or had outlived their usefulness and, as a result, domestic programs, which had been growing rapidly for three decades have finally been contained. . . . Domestic spending, which grew nearly threefold in real terms in little more than two decades, will actually be lower this year than it was in 1981. . . . Eligibility criteria have been tightened to target benefits more to the truly needy, and significant steps have been taken to improve the efficiency and effectiveness of these programs. . . . The nation must ask for no more publicly provided services and benefits than the taxpayers can reasonably be asked to finance.[12]

The values that underlie this message are clearly traditional, an extension of the mood Jordan identified in 1978. Here are the familiar themes of efficiency and self-reliance, embodied in a call for lower domestic spending, rigorous means testing, and a strictly limited government role in social programs.

In terms of fundamental personal attitudes, Americans may be less opposed to social intervention than recent changes in social policy suggest. Just two weeks before the Reagan message quoted above, for instance, 39 percent of the respondents to a *New York Times*/CBS poll said that they thought federal spending on programs for the poor should be kept the same; while an even larger proportion—48 percent—said such spending should be increased; only 8 percent advocated cuts in programs for the poor.[13] Such responses might suggest that values supporting intervention were again on the ascendant.

But when we speak of the predominant values of an era in relation to social welfare, we are not speaking only of citizens' personal inclinations, but of the values that the society as a whole expresses through policy choices and program implementation. Social welfare decisions over the past decade suggest that traditional values, with their emphasis on efficiency and self-reliance, have significantly overshadowed support for social intervention. The 1970s brought comparatively little social legislation, and in the early 1980s the most significant social welfare actions were major funding cuts. In 1982, for example, while unemployment increased and the poverty rate rose to 15 percent, social programs were cut extensively.[14] That year, according to a Bureau of the Census report, 40 percent of the households below the poverty line received neither food stamps nor Medicaid nor housing assistance nor school lunches.[15]

While some state governments moved to pick up at least some of the benefits cut at the federal level, the degree of commitment varied by state, depending, among other things, on the vigor with which provider groups—the health-care industry, social workers, teachers, and others—lobbied for the continuation of their services. Through these efforts, services for the very neediest were generally continued: Nathan et al. report, however, that after 1981 the working poor were almost entirely cut off from public assistance.[16]

For the majority of Americans times improved as 1983 turned to 1984. With inflation falling and employment rising, it was tempting to believe that general prosperity would make other social interventions unnecessary. Yet, at the same time, a growing body of data was making clear that for certain segments of the population, times were not better but worse:

1. A study by the Congressional Joint Committee on Taxation revealed that for the first time in twenty years an increasing number of poor people each year were subject to federal income tax. A family of four at the poverty level, for instance, now had to pay nearly 10 percent of its income in taxes.[17]
2. The Census Bureau's annual report on poverty showed that the percent of people in poverty in 1983 was the highest in eighteen years: 15.2 percent, including 35.7 percent of all blacks and 25 percent of all children under six.[18]
3. A 1984 Congressional Budget Office study of the cumulative effect of tax changes and funding cuts since January 1981 showed the following changes by family income group:
    Incomes below $10,000—Lost, on the average, $390 per year
    Incomes $40,000-$50,000—Gained, on the average, $3,900 per year
    Incomes over $80,000—Gained, on the average, $8,270 per year.[19]

These data did not, however, generate significant support for renewed social intervention. The philosophy that self-discipline and hard work could solve most social problems was expressed repeatedly, and Americans seemed generally satisfied with this approach.

What role does political leadership play in shaping the movement away from social intervention? One 1982 book makes clear its answer in the title: *What Reagan Is Doing to Us.*[20] The truth, of course, goes much deeper. President Reagan, his political talents notwithstanding, espoused ideas that were only a more explicit exposition of trends that had been gaining influence for more than ten years. The present tilt toward traditional values may not express the full range of Americans' personal beliefs, but Americans have supported that tilt collectively since the early 1970s, by both their actions and their inactions. Temporizing values undoubtedly lie within the national consciousness as well and might be evoked under different circumstances. But in recent years traditional values must be judged the most influential in guiding America's approach to social welfare. These values are a fragmenting force in the social welfare institution today. With their heavy emphasis on self-reliance and individual responsibility, they have a tendency to detract from the sense of collective concern on which a cohesive social welfare institution is built.

The Tilt in Technology: Change the Client

Given the tilt toward traditional values which we have just discussed, it is not surprising to find a technological tilt toward rehabilitation. An important theme in social welfare today is that the system is fundamentally sound and that the task of social intervention is simply to equip the disadvantaged to participate more fully in it. This theme was not new with President Reagan, nor President Carter, nor President Ford, nor President Nixon. To some degree, it has always been a part of American thinking, given obvious weight by the fact that indeed millions have benefited from the American system of opportunity, just as it is. With this history in mind, it has not been difficult to conclude that the problem in social welfare is to alter the disadvantaged client so that he or she can benefit from the opportunities the system already provides.

This view of social intervention was noticeably influential in the War on Poverty. The poor were seen, in Henry Aaron's words, "as an afflicted and relatively stable group, suffering from a kind of disease that they were likely to transmit to their children if it were not treated."[21] Phrases like "the culture of poverty," "transmitted deprivation," and "the cycle of poverty" all suggested the existence of an objective disorder that separated—often for life—the individuals who had it from those who did not, and that played an even stronger role than external constraints in keeping those who had it disadvantaged. Many proponents of this view believed that social injustices had contributed to the creation of a deprived underclass; they felt, however, that the chief focus of their programmatic efforts must be the dysfunctional set of characteristics that the disadvantaged client had developed as a result. Because of these characteristics, the provision of direct assistance, such as jobs or cash, was not seen as central. What was needed was for the client to change—socially, educationally, or vocationally.

In the next chapter we will review the specific programs that evolved as a result of this emphasis on rehabilitation during the Great Society years and after. At this point, our principal focus is the overall orientation represented by the programs: the belief that if clients could be made more skillful, more intelligent, more disciplined, they could ensure their own success. Thus, although the rhetoric of the Great Society was reconstructive in tone, leading both its admirers and its detractors to think of it as offering radical reform, much of the legislation that emerged during those years—the Economic Opportunity Act, the Elementary and Secondary Education Act, the Higher Education Act—was fundamentally rehabilitative.

This commitment to rehabilitative technologies has continued with relatively little change. While the *level* of funding has declined, particularly at the federal level, the *kinds* of programs being supported are still primarily rehabilitative. Staff hired under the Jobs and Training Partnership Act of 1982, for instance, are not asked to analyze or change the labor market's ability to absorb the community's unemployed; their charge, rather, is to train the unemployed to fit the needs identified by the area Private Industry Council, a majority of whose members are local businessmen. The client, not the system, is still the focus of intervention. The approach in other areas of social welfare has been similar. Technologies that rehabilitate the client through education or therapy have generally been continued, though at a reduced level, with either state or federal money.

What has *not* received continuing support in recent years has been the more reconstructive side of social welfare technology, the effort to prevent problems through system change and reform. The programs that have been discontinued or altered most significantly in the past decade have tended to be those that focused most visibly on reconstruction: the Civil Rights Commission, Legal Services, the Office of Economic Opportunity, the Community Action Program, the job-creation sections of the Comprehensive Employment and Training Act, and the various programs to create new housing for the poor. In this period of retrenchment and consolidation, even the energies of social activists have tended to be concentrated on protecting the gains won in the past, rather than on breaking new ground. Rehabilitation, not reconstruction, is the predominant focus of social welfare technology today.

This client-specific focus has, on the whole, been detrimental to the cohesion of the social welfare institution. If fifty clients suffer from a dysfunctional system, it is both necessary and practical to look for a common solution to the difficulty. The rehabilitative answer, however, is to focus more on what needs to be remedied in each client. Changing fifty clients may involve fifty different approaches; over time, specialized skills are developed for each one, with distinct credentials, job titles, and professional turf. Rehabilitative technologies thus contribute further to the balkanization of the social welfare institution.

The Tilt in Structure: Power Moves to the States

When traditional values hold center stage and rehabilitative approaches to service are stressed, a tilt toward decentralization is likely to occur as well.

With individual assistance the focus of social welfare, there is little demand for governmental leadership and system-wide reform. President Reagan expressed the point of view most vividly. "You know," he told a crowd in Alabama,

> I've often had a feeling sometimes there in the national Government—I even had it sometimes at the state level, never in my hometown—the feeling that sometimes if we just slipped out, we in government, and closed the doors, turned the key, and disappeared for a while, it would take you a long time to miss us.[22]

Again, it is important to see Reagan as a powerful spokesman for, not the author of, the tilt toward decentralization of the social welfare institution. As we have noted earlier, a deep-seated preference for individual rather than collective action has long been a part of the American way of thinking. Centralized efforts, particularly under governmental direction, have tended to come about only in times of crisis.

The past two decades are often cited as an example of uncontrolled growth at the federal level, but it was federal leadership and federal funding, not federal employment, that grew; the expansion of social programs, though largely paid for with federal dollars, occurred principally at the state and local levels. In 1952 persons employed by the federal government made up 38 percent of the total public payroll; by 1980 the federal share was 17 percent. During these years, federal employment grew 10 percent (much less than the 50 percent increase in overall population), while state and local employment increased 225 percent.[23]

During the 1970s, both President Nixon and President Carter made some unsuccessful efforts in the direction of centralization. There was, for instance, Nixon's proposal for a federal Family Assistance Program to replace the existing welfare system. President Carter made an equally unsuccessful attempt to reform welfare, and failed as well with his proposal for national health insurance. But on the whole both administrations tended to pursue decentralizing approaches and to convey the philosophy that the federal government had little to contribute (except money) to the social welfare institution.

The revenue-sharing initiatives launched by President Nixon in 1969 set the tone for the decade: "After a third of a century of power flowing from the people and the States to Washington, it is time for a New Federalism in which power, funds and responsibility will flow from Washington to the States and to the people."[24] By 1975 several forms of revenue sharing had been passed. A "general" revenue-sharing fund divided $5 billion per year among 39,000 state and local governments, with virtually no restrictions on how the money could be spent. The Comprehensive Employment and Training Act of 1973 grouped a number of existing employment programs together, to be allocated as localities chose; a similar package for community development combined into one fund half a dozen previously separate grants. With the passage of these bills, the trend toward decentralization, begun almost unnoticed in the Great Society years, was confirmed, with one important difference. In the years of the Great Society the federal government remained firmly in the center of the social welfare institution, providing powerful leadership as well as funds; only the process by which programs were implemented was decentralized. Under the New Federalism, leadership was decentralized as well. As Caputo expressed the philosophy:

> The states and local units of government were in fact the levels of government responsible for establishing priorities and creating programs to meet them. The national government's role was to provide financial assistance, but it was up to political leaders at the state and local level to establish priorities, without having excessive restrictions built into the legislation.[25]

The years since 1980 have brought another stage of decentralization, as significantly larger areas of social welfare have been dispersed to the states and federal funding has been substantially reduced. Illustrative of the current trend is the Omnibus Budget Reconciliation Act of 1981. In addition to extensive cuts in federal funding, this bill initiated a dramatic expansion of the revenue-sharing principle. Hundreds of existing federal grants for a wide range of purposes were consolidated into a handful of block grants, the funds within each block to be allocated as states chose. Out of forty-four programs involving federal funds to education, for instance, thirty were grouped together under a single block grant, leaving the states free to cut or discontinue any programs within the block as they wished. Nineteen of twenty-five health programs were consolidated into four block grants, and six social services grants into one block. The effect, as the *Congressional Quarterly* observed, was "a major change in the direction of government."[26]

Increasingly, states have been encouraged to set their own goals, with neither the funding nor the policy direction from Washington to require special concern for areas of significant social need. School districts are being given much wider latitude for "free choice" approaches to desegregation; the reorganized Civil Rights Commission is encouraging the dismantling of affirmative action efforts in which the federal government formerly took the lead; urban areas that counted on Washington's support in their dealings with state legislatures are finding that federal guidelines now offer them little protection; advocacy groups that had formed effective national constituencies are now having to develop separate strategies for each state. This shift of decision making from the federal to the state level has necessarily contributed further to the balkanization of the social welfare institution, as fifty governors and fifty state legislatures develop separate solutions to national problems.

The increasing emphasis on the purchase of social welfare services from the private sector has aggravated the problem further. Whatever the merits of the private sector in terms of speed, efficiency, or service quality,[27] the purchase-of-services approach has greatly complicated the task of ensuring that social needs are met. Hundreds of thousands of providers are involved, with no organizational relationship to those administering the funds. Monitoring of service volume and fiscal accountability may be maintained, but the tremendous diversity and autonomy of the service providers make coherent planning and evaluation extremely difficult. The growing emphasis on voluntarism, also stressed in recent years, has tended to disperse still further the locus of control and accountability. Overall, the increased use of private and voluntary providers has intensified the fragmentation of the social welfare institution.

In all its forms—diminution of the federal leadership role, emphasis on local priority setting, reduction of federal financial support, increased use of the private sector—decentralization has shown a tendency to pull the social welfare institution apart, reinforcing the balkanizing effects of traditional values and rehabilitative technologies.

A Balkanized Institution

As the social welfare institution has become increasingly balkanized, there has been a growing tendency to see each social problem and each social intervention in isolation. Barriers have hardened between levels of government and between agencies. New York is cut off from Mississippi, the psychiatrist from the welfare worker, the white client from the black, and, above all, those who are prospering from those in trouble. Traditional values encourage this separation, with their emphasis on individualism and self-reliance; rehabilitative technologies reinforce it, stressing each client's individual failings rather than shared social needs; decentralized structures formalize it, reducing the constraints of external direction but also reducing the influence of common goals and standards.

More and more, in such a climate, the various segments of the social welfare institution function with little relation to each other. Problems are defined in terms of separate clients, separate agencies, separate states, or separate levels of government. The solutions that emerge reflect the same fragmentation. Balkanization at the staff level results in elaborate differentiation among professional specialties; at the organizational level it encourages a multiplicity of special-purpose agencies, each designed to focus its energies on a narrowly defined spectrum of need.

We have noted the emergence of these balkanizing tendencies in the mid-1960s. Many of the Great Society programs were created for specific recipient groups and encouraged by their very creation a particularist, fragmented view of social welfare. Individual programs were established as political alliances made them possible, often with little regard for the organizational environment in which they would need to operate. Douglass Cater, special assistant for health programs to Lyndon Johnson, describes Johnson as the General George C. Patton of our domestic wars, scoring breakthroughs wherever they could be made and driving as far ahead as possible within the limited time span available to him. He could argue with justice that a president, like a battlefield commander, cannot afford to wait for orderly advance all along the line. Inevitably, the federal breakthroughs were to bring confusion and a degree of chaos in their wake.[28]

The "umbrella" agencies that were created next, in an effort to restore coordination to fragmented services at the state or local level, had little success. Such bodies as the Model Cities agencies, the Comprehensive Area Manpower Planning Systems and the Comprehensive Health Planning agencies (as well as their successors, the Health Systems agencies) all suffered, in McCarthy's words, from "broad goals and limited powers."[29] The language creating the Comprehensive Health Planning agencies serves as an example:

> Federal financial assistance must be directed to support the marshaling of all health resources—national, state and local—to assure comprehensive health services of high quality for every person, but without interference with existing patterns of private professional practice.[30]

In each case, the rhetoric of centralization with which the coordinative agency was created was negated by an unwillingness to make significant changes in the decentralized environment within which it was to operate. Miringoff cites the example of a program serving indigent alcoholics, caught between conflicting efforts of an agency intended to coordinate poverty programs and another coordinating alcoholism services. "At times," he observes, "the only solution appears to be the creation of an agency for coordinating coordinative agencies."[31]

Divided by client type, by funding source, and by service setting, the social welfare institution has become increasingly fragmented over the past decade; its present structure reflects neither the range of problems its clients face nor a rational system for solving them. Roemer's description of American health care applies as well to the social welfare institution as a whole:

> A bewildering array of programs, services and agencies confronts the individual seeking health care in the United States. . . . The complexity of the health service system in the United States is the result of the accretion of programs and agencies over the years as new needs in health services have been recognized, of the specialized and categorical character of these services, of the sheer numbers of individuals and organizations that provide health care, and of the lack of a rational pattern for fitting the many parts in an effective whole.[32]

As the balkanization of the social welfare institution has progressed, it has become more and more difficult to see social issues whole. Constituencies have developed among client groups and among providers, each focusing on their own particular needs and merits. While group solidarity can be a most positive force, the present orientation of the social welfare institution has tended to encourage the more divisive side of such consciousness. The scarcity of financial support in recent years has contributed further to the divisions among these groups, since the zero-sum mentality (if you win, I lose) is reinforced by a sense of competition for the limited resources available. Even where collaboration and coalition would be of obvious value to the groups involved, the atmosphere of recent times has made such collaboration less common.

Meanwhile, the real issues of social welfare remain as broad as ever, crossing all the boundaries that balkanization constructs. Begin to explore why a particular low-income family cannot find housing, and one learns that many low-income families have the same difficulty; begin to explore why, and a hundred interrelated issues emerge—local politics, public assistance funding levels, safety codes, mortgage and insurance practices, landlord/tenant relations, transportation routes, employment opportunities, neighborhood dynamics, and family structure. A social welfare institution that treats each of these issues as separate and unrelated is at a disadvantage, since each issue is only one piece in a puzzle. Solutions are yet more difficult when those seeking housing for *different* low-income groups (welfare families, the elderly, the handicapped) operate in isolation from each other, confronting the same network of problems yet gaining neither insight nor solidarity from each others' efforts. A final level of fragmentation is added in a decentralized system, where each state or locality works in a vacuum, cut off from formal association with all the other states and localities grappling with the same problem.

In recent years, the forces that hold the social welfare institution together have increasingly been subordinated to the forces that tend to pull it apart. At every level, separateness has tended to overshadow cohesion, and the sense of mutual support and common goals that was so essential in periods like the Progressive Era, the New Deal, and, to some extent, the Great Society has begun to disappear. Like the Balkan states, each element of the social welfare institution has come to focus increasingly on its own needs, its own solutions.

We have begun our analysis of the dynamics of social welfare with an overview of current trends in the social welfare institution. In the next two chapters we will examine the practical effects of these trends, first (in Chapter Six) on social programs and then (in Chapter Seven) on individual lives—those of the clients and staff of the social welfare institution.

SUMMARY

Having looked at values, technology, and structure separately in previous chapters, we proceeded here to examine the interactions among the three. Relations among the three were seen to be highly complex, with each element playing a role in how the other two evolve. An example—the development of the Medicare program—was offered in which the interplay among the three elements could be traced.

Trends in values, structure, and technology do not occur randomly; values minimizing social intervention, for instance, are likely to be associated with a tilt toward rehabilitative technologies and decentralized structures. Taking the New Deal as an example, one can observe that values favoring intervention were most influential; these combined naturally with reconstructive technologies and a tendency toward centralized structures.

In the social welfare institution today, traditional values appear to have reemerged, supported by primarily rehabilitative technologies and a strong leaning toward decentralization. Each of these trends separately—and the three of them collectively—are forces that work against the cohesion of the social welfare institution. The result is balkanization, a condition in which the various elements of the social welfare institution, like the warring Balkan states, dissipate their energies and resources instead of working together for common goals.

NOTES

1. Quoted in Henry J. Aaron, *Politics and the Professors: The Great Society in Perspective* (Washington, D.C.: Brookings Institution, 1978), p. 139.

2. See, for instance, Richard J. Murnane, "How Clients' Characteristics Affect Organizational Performance: Lessons from Education," *Journal of Policy Analysis and Management* 2 (3), Spring 1983, pp. 403–417; Edward B. Fiske, "Paying for the Bill for School Reform," *New York Times*, Nov. 13, 1983, sec. 12, p. 1.

3. Robert Morris, *Social Policy of the American Welfare State* (New York: Harper & Row, 1979), p. 88.

4. "Proliferation of All-Payer Systems," *Hospitals*, Apr. 16, 1984, p. 28.

5. Emily Friedman, "A Decisive Decade for HMO's," Ibid., p. 96.

6. ———, "With a Little Help from Their Friends: Blue Cross Plans, with a Hand—Or a Shove—from State Government, Try New Payment Schemes," *Hospitals*, Oct. 1, 1983, p. 80.

7. "Major Corporations Ask Workers to Pay More of Health Cost," *New York Times*, Sept. 12, 1983, p. A1.

8. "Blue Cross Devises Plan to Curb Unneeded Tests," *New York Times*, June 14, 1984, p. B28.

9. "AMA Bids Doctors Voluntarily Freeze Their Fees for a Year," *New York Times*, Feb. 24, 1984, p. A1.

10. "10 Hospitals in New York to Try to Shorten Surgery-Patient Stay," *New York Times*, Nov. 13, 1983, p. A1.

11. Joseph A. Califano, Jr., *Governing America: An Insider's Report from the White House and the Cabinet* (New York: Simon and Schuster, 1981), p. 411.

12. Ronald Reagan, Budget Message, *New York Times*, Feb. 2, 1984, p. B8.

13. *New York Times*/CBS News Poll conducted Jan. 14–21, 1984, *New York Times*, Jan. 29, 1984, p. E1.

14. "Reagan Halted Growth in Noncash Aid Programs," *New York Times*, Sept. 23, 1984, p. B10. See also Dale Tate, "Reconciliation Spending Cut Bill Sent to Reagan," *Congressional Quarterly* 39 (31), Aug. 1, 1981, pp. 1371ff, and "House Ratifies Savings Plan in Stunning Reagan Victory," *Congressional Quarterly* 39 (26), pp. 1127–1129; Ira Moscovice and William Craig, "The

Omnibus Reconciliation Act and the Working Poor,'' *Social Service Review* 58 (1), March 1984, pp. 49-62; ''Many Who Lost Aid Work More but Stay Poor, Study Concludes,'' *New York Times*, Mar. 31, 1984, p. 1; U.S. Conference of Mayors, *Housing Needs and Conditions in America's Cities* and *Homelessness in America's Cities*, cited in *New York Times*, June 16, 1984, p. A7.

15. ''Reagan Halted Growth in Noncash Aid Programs,'' *New York Times*, Sept. 23, 1984, p. B10.

16. Richard P. Nathan, Fred C. Doolittle, and Associates, *The Consequences of Cuts: The Effects of the Reagan Domestic Program on State and Local Governments* (Princeton: Princeton Urban and Regional Research Center, 1983).

17. ''Substantial Rise is Found in Federal Tax Burden on the Poor,'' *New York Times*, Oct. 25, 1983, p. A29.

18. ''Rate of Poverty Found to Persist in Face of Gains,'' *New York Times*, Aug. 3, 1984, p. A1.

19. ''Budget Study Finds Cuts Cost the Poor as the Rich Gained,'' *New York Times*, Apr. 4, 1984, p. A1.

20. See Alan Gartner, Colin Greer, and Frank Riessman, eds., *What Reagan Is Doing to Us* (New York: Harper & Row, 1982). The effects of social and economic policies since 1980 are discussed in detail in John L. Palmer and Isabel V. Sauhill, eds., *The Reagan Experiment: An Examination of Economic and Social Policies under the Reagan Administration* (Washington, D.C.: Urban Institute, 1982); Gartner, Greer, and Riessman, *What Reagan Is Doing to Us*; Joseph A. Pechman, ed., *Setting National Priorities: The 1984 Budget* (Washington, D.C.: Brookings Institution, 1983).

21. Henry J. Aaron, *Politics and the Professors*, p. 34. See also Richard Titmuss, *Commitment to Welfare* (New York: Pantheon, 1968).

22. ''Reagan Telling Crowds '84 is 'Wonderful Time,' '' *New York Times*, July 6, 1984, p. A8.

23. Office of Management and Budget, *Special Analyses of the Budget of the United States* (Washington, D.C.: U.S. Government Printing Office, 1981).

24. Richard M. Nixon, Address to the Nation on Domestic Programs, Aug. 8, 1969, *Public Papers* (Washington, D.C.: U.S. Government Printing Office, 1971), p. 638.

25. David A. Caputo, ''General Revenue Sharing and American Federalism: Towards the Year 2000,'' in David A. Caputo, ed., *General Revenue Sharing and Federalism* (Philadelphia: American Academy of Political Science, 1975), p. 132.

26. ''House Ratifies Savings Plan in Stunning Reagan Victory,'' *Congressional Quarterly* 39 (26), June 27, 1981, pp. 1127-1129; ''Reconciliation Spending Cut Bill Sent to Reagan,'' *Congressional Quarterly* 39 (31), Aug. 1, 1981, pp. 1,371ff.

27. See, for instance, A. J. Culyer, ''Public or Private Health Services: A Skeptic's View,'' *Journal of Policy Analysis and Management* 2 (3), Spring 1983, pp. 386-402; Margaret Gibelman, ''Are Clients Served Better when Services are Purchased?'' *Public Welfare* 39 (4), Fall 1981, pp. 26-33; Neil Gilbert, *Capitalism and the Welfare State* (New Haven: Yale University Press, 1984); Ken Judge and Jillian Smith, ''Purchase of Service in England,'' *Social Services Review* 57 (2), June 1983, pp. 209-233; Bill Jordan, *Freedom and the Welfare State* (London: Routledge & Kegan Paul, 1976); Richard J. Murnane, ''How Clients' Characteristics Affect Organizational Performance: Lessons from Education,'' *Journal of Policy Analysis and Management* 2 (3), Spring 1983, pp. 403-417; Edward Logue, ''The Future for New Housing in New York City,'' in Richard Plunz, ed., *Housing Form and Public Policy in the United States* (New York: Praeger Publishers, 1980), pp. 13-15.

28. Douglass Cater and Philip R. Lee, eds., *Politics of Health* (New York: Medcom Press, 1972), p. 506.

29. Carol McCarthy, ''Planning for Health Care,'' in Steven Jonas and contributors, eds., *Health Care Delivery in the United States* (New York: Springer Publishing Company, 1977), p. 365.

30. Ibid., pp. 359-360.

31. Marc L. Miringoff, *Management in Human Service Organizations* (New York: Macmillan Publishing Co., 1980), p. 199.

32. R. Roemer et al., *Planning Urban Health Services: From Jungle to System* (New York: Springer Publishing Co., 1975), p. 11.

CHAPTER SIX

The Operational Level of Social Welfare: Working Principles and Social Programs

In the previous chapters we discussed how the changing interactions of value, technology, and structure create the social welfare institution; we concluded with a description of how recent trends have moved the social welfare institution increasingly toward balkanization. We will now apply this analysis to the operational level of social welfare.

From the interaction of values, technology, and structure in any given period emerge that era's working principles; these principles determine the actual shape and content of social programs. Working principles rarely appear as written guidelines. Rather, they are a set of underlying (and frequently unspoken) assumptions about how social welfare should work. They follow logically from the overall orientation to social welfare that is shared by the society, but they operate at a much more concrete level. They shape new legislation, they help determine which programs from earlier eras are continued and which are terminated, and they influence the way programs are carried out day to day by human services staff.

The present balkanized pattern of American social welfare has, necessarily, determined the working principles by which today's social programs are shaped. At the operational level, American social welfare seems to be characterized by increasing fragmentation, a growing tendency to look at social problems in isolation from each other. The working principles we have identified reflect this fragmentation, defining social welfare in terms of separate clients, separate episodes of need, and separate program solutions. The principles can be summarized as follows:

Premise 1: Deficiency-oriented intervention. Because the American system of opportunity and rewards is felt to be fundamentally sound, it is assumed that those who display social problems have some deficit that prevents them from fully participating in the system. The focus of social intervention thus becomes to change each individual to where he or she can take advantage of the system's benefits.

Premise 2: Time-limited assistance. Dependence on social intervention is seen as an unnatural condition that should be discontinued as quickly as possible. Social programs are thus expected to be short-term, highly focused, and designed to end as soon as the emergency passes.

Premise 3: Incrementalism. Because there is a preference for using social intervention as sparingly as possible and because strong central control is felt to be outside the American tradition, social welfare programs tend to be created one by one, as local needs and demands indicate, with system-wide planning and development being instituted only as a last resort.

Premise 4: Accountability. To ensure that social intervention is kept to a minimum, in terms of duration, expenditure, and scope, there is a concern that social welfare programs should be rigorously monitored for efficiency and effectiveness. No matter how appealing a program may seem in theoretical or humanitarian terms, it is held accountable for visible practical results.

In this chapter we will explore these working principles and consider how each has shaped the programs that constitute today's social welfare institution.

DEFICIENCY-ORIENTED INTERVENTION

The traditional commitment to individualism and self-reliance is not shaken when social problems are identified in American society. "Most of the time for most people," the credo goes, "individuals in America can make it on their own. What is different about this individual that makes him unable to benefit from the system?" At its best, when temporizing values like compassion are more influential, such an attitude can offer an opportunity for recognizing the separate humanity of each person in need; at its worst, it is simply, in William Ryan's words, "blaming the victim."[1] But in both cases, the task for social intervention becomes to correct individual deficiencies, to fill gaps in a social order that is presumed otherwise to be functioning smoothly. This view of social welfare is well within the American tradition, firmly rooted in the traditional values and rehabilitative policy premises described in earlier chapters.

The tendency to focus on client deficiencies has been strikingly evident in the program approaches of recent years. Let us look at two areas that have been the focus of extensive social intervention: poverty and unemployment.

Poverty Programs

The War on Poverty ended more than a decade ago, but its programs constituted a major element of the social welfare institution throughout the 1970s, and some of the working principles on which they were based remain unquestioned today.

As we noted in Chapter Five, the rehabilitative orientation of much of the antipoverty legislation has sometimes been overlooked because the language in which it was presented took a much more reconstructive tone. When the Economic Opportunity Act, for example, was described in its preamble as being designed to "eliminate the paradox of poverty in the midst of plenty in this Nation,"[2] it suggested massive social reform. Only an analysis of the actual programs involved makes clear that the plan for eliminating poverty rested primarily, not on changing social systems that affected the poor, but on improving the ability of the poor to participate in the *existing* system. As Miringoff explains in detail, remediation of individual clients' deficiencies was the central focus of many of the Economic Opportunity Act programs—Job Corps, Neighborhood Youth Corps, Work Study, Adult Basic Education, and Work Experience.[3] Even the primarily reconstructive Community Action Program had as one of its three goals the task of improving "human performance, motivation and productivity."[4] The same principles are identifiable in much of the subsequent Great Society legislation intended to help the poor, including Head Start, Upward Bound, and the Elementary and Secondary Education Act. All in all, more than sixty education and training bills were passed during the few years of the Great Society, each dedicated to the unspoken principle that one important way of attacking poverty was to help the poor overcome their deficiencies.

Friedman observes that focusing on client deficiencies had its practical side. Three choices for attacking poverty were available in 1965, he says: providing increased transfer payments, changing social structures, or changing the poor. The first was too expensive, the second was too controversial, so the choice fell to the third—changing the poor.[5] While this explanation understates the intellectual and psychological appeal of the deficiency-oriented focus, it does suggest the practical difficulties that would have arisen had any other approach been chosen. What began as a war on *poverty* turned rapidly into something less controversial: a crusade for equal *opportunity*. The programs actually enacted settled for even less: Many of them focused almost exclusively on preparing the poor to take better advantage of the opportunities that already existed.

While the glowing promises and expansive federal role of the Great Society were soon discredited, programs for the poor remained relatively the same throughout the 1970s. A few were phased out, but many continued until late in the decade, silent testimony to the continuing appeal of the deficiency-focused principles on which they were based. Head Start, Job Corps, Work Study, and compensatory education programs for students of various ages all were continued; all suggested that an effective way of fighting poverty was to improve the poor.

With the funding cuts and block grants of the 1980s, most of the poverty programs disappeared. The new approach to poverty was enunciated by President Reagan in a speech to Republican women officeholders in 1984: "Today our nation has one big program to help every American—man, woman and child. It's called economic recovery."[6] The special needs of the poor continued to come to public attention, however, and when they did, public response tended once more to focus on client deficiencies. Now the deficiencies appeared to be more those of character and motivation than of skills. In recent years it has been suggested, for example, that many of the nation's homeless are in that condition "by choice";[7] that "people go to soup kitchens because the food is free and that's easier than paying for it";[8] that federal spending for education (which had been targeted principally on programs for the poor) is less important than "good old-fashioned discipline," removing drug and alcohol abuse from the schools, and raising academic standards;[9] and that "if we strengthen families, we'll help reduce poverty and the whole range of other social problems."[10] While not all Americans would subscribe explicitly to those statements, the social programs of the 1980s have expressed a similar viewpoint. Those programs most specifically focused on clients' deficiencies, such as the array of mental health, counseling, and rehabilitative services, have generally continued, whereas programs that simply provided assistance with daily life—food stamps, welfare, legal services, day-care, housing—have been cut back, either through reduced funding or tightened eligibility. In the 1980s, more than ever, the focus on client deficiencies is central to the implementation of social welfare.

Employment Programs

When the issue of client deficiencies has arisen, few shortcomings have received as much attention as the inability or unwillingness to hold a job. Turning the disadvantaged into reliable wage earners has always been an important feature of American social programs, whether they served the mentally ill, the handicapped, juvenile delinquents, ex-offenders, or the poor. Theodore Roosevelt set the tone very early: "Able-bodied tramps and paupers must work."[11] Nearly a century later, Richard Nixon's 1968 acceptance speech at the Republican Convention in Miami sounded the same theme: "For those who are able to help themselves, what we need are not more millions on the welfare rolls, but more millions on the payrolls in the United States."[12] Every recent administration has stressed the idea that employable members of society must be pressed to participate in the competitive labor market.

It is probably significant that the only time in which job creation has been a major aspect of manpower policy was during the Depression, when it seemed clear that recipients' unemployment was not their fault. For there is an important difference between focusing exclusively on competitive employment and providing public sector jobs as well. The former is based on the assumption that work is available if the client can be trained or forced to find it. A program of public employment, on the other hand, implies that government participation may also be necessary to provide the type or number of jobs needed.

One employment initiative that lasted throughout the 1970s was the Work Incentive Program (WIN). It required AFDC recipients judged to be employable to register for training or jobs as a condition of receiving their benefits. As such, it stressed clients' deficiencies in two ways. First, it suggested, like the other training programs we have discussed, that lack of training was the principal obstacle to employment for AFDC recipients. Second, its compulsory features added the suggestion that recipients' deficiencies included unwillingness to work as well as lack of training. Unemployment was thus attacked through a program that addressed recipients' moral deficiencies (unwillingness to work) as well as their vocational deficiencies (lack of skills). Program outcomes have not been particularly successful. The first major screening of 2.3 million AFDC recipients for WIN, for example, resulted in referrals of 400,000 to the program. In a follow-up about two years later, only 24,000 (1 percent of the original group) had been employed as long as three months.[13] System problems, like the unavailability of day-care services, the scarcity of jobs, and the strong disincentives for work built into the welfare benefit structure, have so far significantly outweighed the impact of trying to attack joblessness through either training or forced registration.

The principal piece of manpower legislation during the 1970s was the Comprehensive Employment and Training Act (CETA), passed in 1973 and amended in 1974 and 1978. This elaborate bill included the training-oriented programs of the War on Poverty (Job Corps, Neighborhood Youth Corps, Operation Mainstream, New Careers) and various public employment initiatives, which were folded in as time passed (Emergency Employment Act of 1971, Emergency Jobs and Unemployment Assistance Act of 1974).[14] Even in the public employment portions of CETA, however, the deficiency-oriented approach remained, evidenced, for instance, by the rigorous limits set on participation. Eligibility was restricted more and more tightly as the decade progressed, ensuring that only the very neediest were provided with public jobs. In addition, participation was time limited; again, this linked public employment to deficiency-oriented intervention, since the justification for the time limitation was that clients would develop skills during their period of public employment that they could then use to find competitive work. Public employment, therefore, was offered not simply because it provided needed jobs, but because it helped workers improve their deficient skills.

CETA's dual approach to manpower policy, combining training with job creation, ended in 1982 when CETA was phased out, to be replaced by the new Job Partnership Training Act (JPT). JPT provides no funds for job creation or public employment; its sole purpose is to train the unemployed to fill positions identified by Private Industry Councils in each area.[15] These groups are composed of representatives from business, labor, education, and the community; a majority of the council, as well as the chairman, must be local businessmen. Eligibility to participate in JPT is restricted to the very needy (participants must have incomes below the poverty level, be on welfare, or be receiving food stamps); however, the supportive services that these groups might require, such as day-care and subsistence payments during training, are held to a minimum. Under JPT, the client's skills are the principal focus, and training is virtually the only intervention. People are jobless, the theory goes once more, because they lack the skills or the self-discipline to take advantage of existing opportunities. The task of employment programs is either to instill the deficient self-discipline through tighter enforcement or to augment the deficient skills through additional training.

We have chosen the examples of poverty and unemployment to illustrate how one working principle—deficiency-oriented intervention—has helped to shape the social programs of recent years. Numerous other examples could have been chosen: Mental health services, for instance, focus principally on mental illness; health care is generally for the sick; individualized educational programs are most often initiated for those with learning disabilities; discussions of "the family" often tend to be limited to issues of abortion, illegitimacy, abuse, and divorce. No one of these areas is an inappropriate concern for social welfare; when resources are limited, it is, of course, reasonable to focus one's greatest efforts where they are needed most.

There are, however, some dangers in an exaggerated emphasis on deficiency-oriented intervention. First, this viewpoint can blind those who work in the social welfare institution to the strengths and resources of those they serve. Second, such an emphasis can lead workers to underestimate or overlook the structural factors that contribute to the problems they are trying to solve; in technological terms, it can lead them to stress rehabilitation at the expense of reconstruction. These tendencies, if overdone, can contribute further to the balkanization of the social welfare institution; their suggestion that social problems are primarily the result of individual failures and deficiencies tends to diminish the kinds of mutual support and shared solutions that are essential features of a vital and effective social welfare institution.

TIME-LIMITED INTERVENTION

There was one period in America's history when the tendency to ascribe social problems to individual flaws was markedly reduced: the Depression. In the face of nationwide calamity, it seemed very clear that circumstances, as much as personal failure, could cause deprivation. Yet traditions die hard, and individual self-reliance was still central to the American value system. The problem for President Roosevelt—both a political one in terms of generating public support and a psychological one inasmuch as he shared many of the same views as the electorate he hoped to move—was how to square widespread federally funded public assistance with the historic American distaste for anything that smacked of "the dole."

The answer, which has served the country ever since, was to view the provision of assistance as temporary, emergency relief that would be discontinued as soon as the situation returned to normal. Thus, the section of the original Social Security Act creating Aid to Dependent Children (ADC) was presented as an interim measure to tide widows and orphans of wage earners over until the act's long-term benefits were fully in place. Senator Lister Hill reminisced years later about those assumptions: "I remember when we passed the Act in 1935, the thinking was that the public assistance grants were being only for more or less of a temporary period, that soon everybody would be under OASI and you would not have any need for public assistance grants."[16]

Nearly half a century later, a 1980 report by the Social Security Administration showed that more than 3 million families, with more than 7 million children, were still being supported by this program, now titled Aid for Families of Dependent Children (AFDC).[17] Millions more Americans receive federal support in the form of public housing, medical care, educational assistance, or food stamps. Yet, in spite of the scope and longevity of these programs, there is a continuing reluctance to see them as permanent. Instead, the preference is and has always been to look at each program as a separate time-limited effort to resolve a specific temporary problem.

Richard Nixon's radio speech in 1971 describing welfare payments as a ''temporary expedient'' was presented as an argument for his proposed Family Assistance Plan, which he said would end ''the custodial approach which began with the New Deal.'' [18] Yet part of what opponents objected to about the Family Assistance Plan was that it appeared to institutionalize cash payments to the poor; in spite of the work requirements in the bill—which antagonized would-be supporters on the left—the plan was seen by the right as being too much like guaranteed income.

The hostility to guaranteed income, negative income tax, and other systematized methods of public assistance is deeply influenced, it seems clear, by the continuing American principle that it would be bad policy—and almost bad luck—to establish too stable or generous a system of public assistance. In the American system of social welfare, programs are intended to give one a hand over the rough spots. Solid citizens find the idea of perpetual dependence distasteful, and they count on recipients to feel the same way. One of the unspoken criteria for public services is, as we have noted earlier, that the circumstances under which they are provided should never be so attractive as to make people use them if they have an alternative. The recommendations of England's Poor Law Report in 1834 set a similar tone:

> to provide the necessaries of life, but nothing more, to keep them closely to work, and in all respects under such restrictions, that though no man who was really in want would hesitate for a moment to comply with them, yet he would submit to them no longer than he could help. [19]

Only where programs are closely linked to disability, age, or past salary contributions—as in Social Security—has America accepted the concept of a stable long-term structure of social welfare.

The principle of time-limited assistance can be seen at work in many of today's social welfare programs. Sometimes, as in the process of utilization review in hospitals, it is focused primarily on preventing the overuse of expensive or high-intensity services. In other cases, assistance is time limited for more philosophical reasons, as in the continuing effort to move public assistance recipients off the welfare rolls. While fiscal considerations play a part, they are reinforced by a value-based reluctance to prolong dependency on social programs any longer than absolutely necessary. Finally, time-limited assistance can also occur when the pattern of services is so diverse and uncoordinated that each component focuses exclusively on its own limited interventions.

Let us examine two recent examples of time-limited assistance: eligibility review for disability recipients and the development of programs for the homeless.

Disability Reviews

In recent years, even benefits for the disabled have been affected by the growing preference for time-limited assistance. Acting on guidelines established late in the Carter administration, the Social Security Administration began in 1981 to review the eligibility of all clients receiving Social Security Disability Insurance (SSDI) benefits. SSDI, begun in 1956, provides monthly support payments to those who cannot work because of a mental or physical disability. The standards set by the Social Security Administration for assessing inability to work are explicit and rigorous:

> A person must be not only unable to do his or her previous work or work commensurate with the previous work in amount of earnings and utilization of capacities but cannot, considering age, education, and work experience, engage in any other kind of substantial gainful work which exists in the national economy. It is immaterial whether such work exists in the immediate area, or whether a specific job vacancy exists, or whether the worker would be hired if he or she applied for work.[20]

The purpose of the disability reviews begun in 1981 was to determine how many of those receiving SSDI benefits could be discontinued on the grounds that they were no longer too disabled to work. By the winter of 1984, 1.2 million reviews had been performed, and 491,000 recipients had been removed from the SSDI rolls. Many of the terminated recipients appealed, and the results were dramatic. Of the 371,000 who had been granted judicial hearings by August 1984, more than 200,000 had been ordered reinstated.[21]

Meanwhile, the manner and speed of the termination process were receiving sweeping criticism from a variety of sources. Critics pointed to the fact that recipients first learned that their cases were being reviewed when they received written notification that their benefits had been terminated. They observed that program regulations allowed for only a three-month extension of benefits while appeals were being pursued, although in many states the appeal process took three or four times that long. They expressed concern that the stress of the termination process would be a particular hardship for the many mentally ill and retarded; reports of homelessness and even death as a result of the cutoffs began to circulate. Most of all, critics maintained that Social Security staff were seriously wrong in maintaining that the clients involved were ready to resume work. Many of them had not worked for years; some had had as many as forty psychiatric hospitalizations;[22] others were significantly retarded or physically handicapped.

By the spring of 1984, forty-five states were under court order to stop cutting off benefits until Congress devised fairer standards for the review process. When the Department of Health and Human Services refused to comply, fifteen states announced that they would no longer cooperate with the federal government in removing people from the benefit rolls.[23] "I am being forced to weigh federal mandates versus fair and equitable treatment of my citizens," said Governor White of Texas.[24] Finally, in April 1984, the Department of Health and Human Services agreed to place a moratorium on eligibility denials until new regulations were issued by Congress.

Certain aspects of this episode are dramatic and unusual. It is uncommon to see such sweeping application of an eligibility review process, or such unanimous criticism of the results, or such a high percentage of reversals. But in more important ways, the case of the SSDI denials is simply an exaggerated example of the traditional American antipathy to stable long-term support. In education, in welfare, in mental health, in alcohol and drug counseling, in child guidance, in marital counseling, and in dozens of other fields, there is an inherent tendency—which has intensified in recent years—to become impatient with social problems that do not resolve themselves promptly. The overzealous cancellation of SSDI benefits was in some senses not unlike the frequent eligibility testing that accompanies other social welfare programs—all based on the belief that self-reliance is the norm to which each person should be returned as quickly as possible. Some types of intervention may be required on a consistent long-term basis as an integral part of American social welfare; if so, this concept has not yet been incorporated into the working principles that now shape the nation's social programs.

Programs for the Homeless

The homeless emerged in recent years as another group whose problems raised questions about the scope and duration of social intervention. No one knew how many there were; estimates ranged between 250,000 and 2 million.[25] But in the fall and winter of 1983–84, nearly every American city was grappling with the problem of serving the homeless. Hundreds of churches, coalitions, individuals, voluntary agencies, and governmental offices across the country became involved. Shelters and soup kitchens were set up; food and clothes were collected by volunteers; hospitals tried to meet the critical physical needs of those who came to do screening and counseling in the shelters; caseworkers wrestled with the fact that clients could not qualify for welfare without a permanent address; school districts became used to seeing "hotel kids" arrive and depart as their families were moved from one welfare hotel to the next.

The activity was intense, involving the participation of thousands of groups and individuals across the country. In some respects, the response was a remarkable example of grass-roots social welfare, responding directly and voluntarily to a major social problem. But it was also possible to conclude, as one reviewed the growing body of studies and anecdotal reports, that the majority of programs were short-term and temporary. That this kind of help was needed was undeniable; the question was whether it alone could make a significant dent in the problem.

Kim Hopper, a research associate with the Community Service Society of New York City, drew up a list of some of the principal factors leading to the marked increase in homelessness:

1. Massive depopulation of state mental hospitals, typically accompanied by poor planning for the residential needs of ex-patients once released into the community
2. Continuing high rates of joblessness among low-skilled workers, the drying-up of spot-labor markets, and the slow rise of double-digit unemployment in areas and industries previously considered "recession-proof"
3. A housing crisis characterized by soaring rents, depressed construction, and widespread abandonment, arson, and deterioration of low-income buildings in particular.[26]

In spite of these large-scale social issues, the programs that the social welfare institution has so far provided for the homeless consist almost entirely of temporary shelter, emergency medical care, and some efforts at short-term counseling. Many of the clients involved are indifferent or resistant to the help they are offered; some are also dirty or rude or drunk or violent or wholly withdrawn. John Coleman, the president of Haverford College, studied the problems of the homeless by living as a vagrant on the streets of New York City. He reminisced later about standing in a crowd of street people watching the reactions of middle-class people on their way into Madison Square Garden: "I sensed how uncomfortable they were at the presence of the homeless. Easy to love in the abstract, not so easy face to face."[27]

Yet, while recognizing the challenge that the homeless present to care givers, it does seem possible to suggest that once again the American social welfare institution has chosen to provide scattered time-limited services rather than devoting the resources and time necessary for a more systematic and far-reaching attack on some of the fundamental problems involved. Herbert Blumer has described a five-step process through which a social problem evolves: (1) emergence, when the problem reaches public attention; (2) legitimation, in which recognized authorities acknowledge its validity; (3) mobilization of forces to attack; (4) development of an official "solution"; and (5) implementation of the approved plan. Once implementation occurs, Blumer says, the problem is "solved" in the public's mind, whether or not the difficulties it represents are actually eliminated. Mark Stern applies Blumer's model to the issue of homelessness, tracing the problem through each of Blumer's stages. In terms of community perceptions, according to Stern, the provision of temporary food and shelter has become the official "solution" to the problems of the homeless; now that programs exist to provide these, he says, homelessness has been "solved" and has lost its potency as a public issue.[28]

Considering the American preference, especially in recent years, for time-limited solutions, it is not surprising that program responses to the problems of the homeless have so far been limited to short-term emergency care. But it is important to note how many aspects of the problem this "solution" leaves untouched.

The two examples we have reviewed have shown quite different sides of the instinct for time-limited intervention. In the example of disability denials, the commitment to short-term care led to arbitrary and sometimes destructive administrative decisions that cut off clients' access to benefits. In the case of programs for the homeless, there was considerable evidence of personal caring and commitment to the needs of a difficult population. Yet in some respects the effects of short-term intervention were similar in the two cases. In both examples, and in others that could be cited, the focus on short-term services may have done an injustice to the complexity of the problem being addressed. Both the disabled and the homeless (as well as the mentally ill, the alcoholic, the unemployed, the illiterate, and so on) have needs that are unlikely to be resolved quickly or easily; programs that offer only short-term services run the risk of creating a fragmented and incomplete system of care. In this sense, time-limited interventions make their own contribution to balkanization by encouraging a series of brief and limited services rather than contributing to one well-integrated system.

INCREMENTALISM

Fragmentation of the social welfare institution can come about through limitations on the duration of programs (time-limited assistance) or through limitations on the scope of their planning and development (incrementalism). To understand incrementalism, let us begin by considering its more familiar predecessor, rational planning.

Rational Planning and Incrementalism

In rational planning, as described by Alfred Kahn, a problem is identified and carefully defined, the universe of choices is reviewed, the likely consequences of each choice are explored, and the most productive course of action is selected.[29] In its purest form this model is rarely encountered in daily life, but the disciplined and creative process it describes sets a useful standard for social planning and policymaking.

An alternative to rational planning, offered by Lindblom, has been given the title "incrementalism," although it is more vividly described by its author as "the science of muddling through."[30] Lindblom's argument is that most decision makers have neither the information nor the mandate to do the exhaustive analysis called for in rational planning. Instead, he suggests, they will do better to limit their field of review to the choices involving the least amount of change from present policies, since these are the only changes that are likely to win the necessary support. ''Democracies change their policies almost entirely through incremental adjustments,'' he says. ''Policy does not move in leaps and bounds.''[31]

Whatever the merits of rational planning, it is incrementalism that has predominated recently as a policy premise in American social welfare. The recent trends toward rehabilitative rather than reconstructive technologies and toward decentralized structures have created a climate in which incrementalism follows logically, since these trends tend to encourage small-scale problem-specific approaches and to shy away from system-level planning or reform. In fact, given the working principles we have already discussed in this chapter—a focus on clients' individual deficiencies and an insistence that interventions be time limited—it would be surprising to find enthusiasm for the broad conceptualizations envisioned in rational planning.

Instead, social welfare development seems to proceed almost informally, with new programs or departments being created as new problems emerge and old programs being dropped as funds are cut without any systematic review of what is being offered and how it might be restructured. Rarely is there a planned-out refocusing of funds and energies across a range of agencies or departments.

The assumption that the overall social system is sound and that problems are attributable to those who suffer them is, of course, closely linked to the incremental approach. Following this logic, social problems tend to be viewed separately, each to be dealt with through specialized services, rather than as possible indicators of system-wide dysfunction. If five men are unemployed, for instance, their difficulties are likely to be seen as five separate problems, perhaps calling for five different programs. Of course, attention to the difficulties of individual clients is an important and relevant aspect of social welfare; the concern is that when this focus overshadows all other issues, certain kinds of solutions are excluded from consideration.

The Effect on Shared Planning

Incrementalism affects how programs evolve at all levels of government, as well as in the private sector. In the field of counseling, for example, an assumption has developed that significantly different technologies are involved in counseling children, teenagers, adults, the elderly, drug abusers, alcoholics, the mentally retarded with emotional problems, rape victims, the unemployed, teenage mothers, families, dialysis patients, child abusers, battered wives, the bereaved, and the dying. Accordingly, separate programs have tended to develop for each group, with separate (and often competitive) sources of support. Certainly each of these conditions brings its own stresses, but a close review of the various services provided suggests that there is more common ground than the fragmented programs would suggest. And if the programs are similar, there can be a significant advantage in looking at them as a single system, more in the style of rational planning, rather than adding new programs one by one on an incremental basis and running the obvious risks of service gaps and duplication.

The effort to meet specialized housing needs is another example of how incrementalism can discourage shared planning. There has been a growing tendency over the past twenty years to create residences for particular groups of clients, often with little coordination across agencies. Because the requirements of such housing have been similar—big enough to accommodate a number of clients, not too expensive, and within reach of community services—it has been common for such housing to cluster in less expensive urban neighborhoods. Thus, a single block may find itself with a senior citizen apartment, a residence for released mental patients, a family-care home for a local VA hospital, a halfway house for alcoholics, a group home for juvenile offenders, and a residence for the mentally retarded. Perhaps each agency would rather have had its residence in a more heterogeneous neighborhood, but since each defined its program in terms of its clients' personal characteristics rather than in terms of their shared need for housing, no integrated planning took place.

In a given community, ten or twelve or twenty different agencies may work separately on a generic problem like housing for their clients. Through informal networks, some degree of coordination may occur, but it is rare that organizational policies facilitate this coordination; more commonly they obstruct it. Each client group has individual problems that can and should be addressed, but programs that focus only on these individual problems may miss the opportunity to plan together regarding the larger issues affecting the quality of life for all citizens, and particularly the more vulnerable ones.

Housing is not the only area where greater coordination and more systematic planning could be helpful. When the extensive releases of mental patients into the community began in the 1960s, many of the services found to be needed were those that other community residents had required for a long time. Housing with access for the frail and the handicapped, inexpensive public transportation, skilled nursing care, supervised living facilities, day programs, nutrition services—such programs were frequently created specifically for the mentally ill and then re-created separately at considerable expense for the mentally retarded, the elderly, recovering alcoholics, and other client groups. As always, the emphasis on particular client characteristics rather than shared need was expressed in incrementalism rather than joint planning.

The Effect on Reform

In the examples above, we have seen how an overemphasis on incrementalism can discourage coordinated planning for client groups whose needs overlap. An associated danger is that the exclusive focus on those program options that represent the least change and therefore appear the most politically feasible may decrease the likelihood that efforts toward more ambitious social reform will ever be undertaken. There are obvious incentives in any case for focusing on minor adjustments rather than radical change; incrementalism reinforces those incentives. It is always easier to add a new program than to reform an entrenched system, but it is not always more productive. As different groups in need of employment are iden.ified, for instance, programs multiply, each designed to address the particular characteristics that make it hard for this kind of person to find work. Yet the responsiveness of the American labor market to people whose personal characteristics or work requirements are outside the usual range is a problem that affects the young, the elderly, the handicapped, the poor, women, mothers, students, ex-offenders, those with outmoded skills, and many others. An incremental approach, which encourages addressing each of these groups separately, makes it less likely that some of the underlying problems they all face will be confronted.

Another example of how incrementalism can obscure more fundamental questions can be seen in the effort to integrate handicapped children into regular classrooms. When this initiative began, the problems encountered were treated as brand new, and many of the solutions developed were tailored specifically to the handicaps of the children involved. Yet the underlying difficulty of making educational settings responsive to individual differences continued as a system-wide problem, one that was also being faced by slow learners, gifted children, teenage mothers, adult illiterates, non-English speakers, and a host of others who did not easily fit into the standard classroom groupings. To some extent the problems encountered by each of these groups were only a more dramatic example of a certain rigidity of format that affects many children in school. Again, an incremental approach focusing on each new problem as it arises tends to obscure the commonality of problems across groups.

Perhaps no more vivid example of the price of incrementalism exists than the public assistance program. Federal regulations regarding AFDC and other assistance programs have repeatedly been revised, expanded, cut, and amended; meanwhile, the states have added their own standards and requirements. One of the Studies in Public Welfare issued by the Joint Economic Committee of Congress in 1972 observed: "It is no longer possible—if indeed it ever was—to provide a convincing rationale for the programs as they exist, in terms of who is covered and who is excluded, benefit amounts, and eligibility conditions. No coherent rationale binds them together as a system." [32] Later studies showed the same patterns. In 1976 the annual administrative cost per AFDC case ranged from $130 in Ohio to $430 in Oklahoma; [33] the number of eligibility cases handled per staff member was 42 in Illinois and 146 in Wisconsin;[34] the average monthly payment for a family of four was $60 in Mississippi, $320 nationwide, and $533 in Hawaii.[35]

In recent years the problem has been aggravated by federal cuts in assistance, leaving each state even more on its own. The varying availability in different states of services such as Medicaid, food stamps, school lunch, public housing and day-care, plus differences in the definition and computation of work-related expenses, now mean a difference of hundreds of dollars in the assistance available to poor families with similar incomes across the country. In welfare, as in employment and education, incremental change may solve isolated problems, but it brings the system no closer to the broader reforms that are needed.

The Effect on Structure

America's traditional regard for diversity and free choice has helped to contribute to the patchwork of agencies and programs that today constitute the American social welfare institution. The range and vitality of different programs are evidence of the generosity of American citizens and of their eagerness to be active participants in the effort toward general social well-being. But without rational planning and coordination, such individual efforts can be scattered and duplicative. There are good reasons for the lively amalgam of public and private services that together form the social welfare institution, and it is not likely to disappear. The problem is that the disparate elements within it have never been merged into a single coherent system for meeting the nation's social needs. Once the idea of working with private providers is accepted, it seems, there is a reluctance to impose any kind of rationalizing structure. Private agencies under government contract have been held to standards of fiscal and programmatic accountability, but there has been little emphasis on requiring them to coordinate their efforts with other providers.

As we have seen, programs in the public sector are not much better integrated. The various levels of government—federal, state, county, and municipal—have also developed incrementally, and their various elements can be as duplicative and contentious as competing private agencies. In thirty states, for instance, programs for the aging are administered by a department separate from that which provides welfare programs for other age groups.[36] The reason for this separation is not hard to deduce: Funding for the elderly came through different legislation, at different times, and with different sources of political support. In a climate of incrementalism, these factors are quite enough to justify a freestanding department. The result is that any effort to address the many needs that elderly people share with other age groups must be negotiated across both fiscal and administrative boundaries. Program separation is often associated too with differentiation of technology; the particularism we have discussed earlier in this book is thus reinforced, confirming the feeling that the needs of the aging require separate programs and separate skills.

The way veterans' services are organized is an even clearer instance of balkanization, and again it is attributable to the incremental evolution of separately funded, separately supported programs for specific client-groups—in this case, veterans. Only four states in the country bring veterans' programs and those for the elderly under the same administrative umbrella.[37] Yet the nation's veterans form one of the most significant groups of elderly people, and caring for them over the next two decades will be a major part of the country's effort for the aging. In 1981 there were 3.3 million veterans over the age of sixty-five; by the year 2000 the number is expected to reach 9 million.[38] It is most unlikely that the existing system of VA services will be adequate to respond to this surge in need for hospitals, mental health care, and day programs, yet the present organization of services, which treats veterans as a wholly separate group, tends to discourage the very integration of planning and programs that is essential to develop appropriate solutions.

Many states have established new "umbrella" human service departments that contain within them a range of formerly separate departments. This effort clearly represents a recognition of the problems we have been discussing, since it typically brings under one administrative roof a variety of offices that previously would have had no formal linkage. Yet within these superagencies, the previous incrementally developed structure remains relatively unchanged: Each former department retains its old identity under the umbrella, along with its old boundaries and specialized focus. Children and families are served by one division, the mentally ill by another, and the blind by another. And many essential services remain separate. Housing and employment, for instance, are nearly always administered outside the human service superagency, as are health services in thirty-two states, vocational rehabilitation in twenty-five, and alcohol counseling in twenty-six.[39] Yet it is the need for exactly these programs that so often drives the human service agency's clients to seek help.

Even when staff of different departments try to work together, the fragmentizing effect of incremental public policies, developed at different times by different groups with insufficient consideration of the shared environment in which they must operate, makes rational coordination difficult. As we have noted, the underlying belief that social programs—particularly those in the public sector—are interim arrangements still lingers in America's approach to social planning. There seems to be a deep-seated reluctance to make the kind of integrated long-term commitment to social intervention that would be implied by a major systemization of the nation's various inconsistent social programs. As a result, programs are patched up rather than reformed, with periodic additions, cuts, amendments, and new guidelines that reflect temporary alliances and emergencies more than any unified overview of social needs.

Perhaps the most effective coordination of state-level social welfare has taken place in the area of income maintenance. Many states have established special integrated divisions to administer a whole range of such programs—food stamps, AFDC, SSI, Medicaid, and other forms of financial aid—despite their varied funding sources and the wide range of clients they serve.[40] Integration is not complete: Special assistance for energy costs, for instance, is still provided through a separate office in seventeen states. However, in the area of income maintenance, more than in any other, we see a model of how a coordinated structure can be created. Here, almost alone, states have ignored the historical and political origins of a variety of programs and instead looked freshly at their functions. This example, however, is the exception. In nearly every other service category, incrementalism has resulted in a balkanized approach to the design of social welfare programs.

ACCOUNTABILITY

In a balkanized and fragmented system, it is perhaps natural that a concern for accountability should become increasingly influential in determining how social welfare programs are being carried out. Significant sums are being expended, yet there is neither the philosophical nor the administrative continuity to ensure that what is being done is consistent with what is needed. Ideally, this concern would inspire an effort to improve the coherence and continuity of the overall system of social welfare, so that purposes and approaches could be more clearly defined. In practice, as we have shown, the forces discouraging continuity are very strong; since clarifying purposes has proved so difficult, the tendency instead has been to focus with increasing narrowness on the processes by which social welfare is carried out. In particular, *efficiency* has come to overshadow *effectiveness* as a criterion for judging social programs.

The Evaluation of Social Programs

To some extent, the emphasis on efficiency rather than effectiveness is understandable, given the intangible qualities of much social intervention. In social welfare, program effectiveness is extraordinarily difficult to measure. Ordinarily in program evaluation, one identifies program goals and defines measurable objectives that serve as indicators of progress toward the goals selected. Even these simple steps, however, are difficult in the area of social welfare. What outcome is sought, and how will you know when it has occurred? Is the goal of a program for unwed mothers to ensure that they receive needed services during pregnancy or to help them choose between keeping their babies and giving them up? Is the goal of an alcoholism program to have its clients stay sober for a given length of time or to hold onto their jobs and families or to gain insight into their use of alcohol? When a client leaves a counseling program after six sessions, is that success because he or she no longer feels the need of support or failure because the client is resisting treatment?

Where the program involves one of the more intensive service settings—hospital, residential treatment center, juvenile detention facility, retardation institution—sometimes it seems enough to stipulate that the client will be released to a less restrictive setting. But even the most cursory review of case histories tells us that such a goal is incomplete by itself. Was the released person able to get a job? Could he or she keep the job? Was the individual able to resume relationships with friends and family? What was his or her emotional condition? Each of these questions raises further difficulties of measurement, data collection, and consensus on criteria. Is getting a job a measure of social functioning? Or is job retention a better measure? For how long? How does one measure the viability of family relationships? What is the best indicator of the client's emotional health? Does the question of whether the client is readmitted to a more intensive setting outweigh all these social functioning measures? If the client is not readmitted, does that necessarily mean success? Has the client left town? Has the ex-alcoholic been arrested? Is the ex-convict in a mental hospital?

Some of the major government evaluations of social programs illustrate how difficult it is to verify program achievement. Initial studies of Head Start, for instance, suggested that children who had attended the program did not fare significantly better in subsequent schooling than those who went straight to kindergarten.[41] Later studies, under different auspices, did show some benefit, but the methods and criteria of the various studies were so at variance with each other that it was extremely difficult to compare the findings and use either to refute the other. Evaluations of Job Corps, CETA, WIN, various special education efforts, and housing initiatives presented the same difficulty; different studies arrived at different findings, with so little common ground that no consensus seemed possible.[42]

One of the reasons for the lack of commonality is that external (and frequently uncontrollable) factors can play a decisive role in program outcome. If these uncontrolled variables are excluded, important factors are left out of the analysis; on the other hand, if these variables are built in, they involve such dense and complex interactions that it is hard to know what the findings mean. The 1970s saw two examples of this problem: an experiment on negative income tax[43] and another on providing the poor with vouchers for housing rather than accommodating them in subsidized units.[44] Both these massive multi-year experiments were technically sophisticated, with a tremendous variety of variables built into the program design. The results were as intricate as the experiments, drawing on a whole range of different settings and experimental conditions. Unfortunately, because of just this sophistication, the findings were so complicated that proponents of nearly every point of view found something in the reports to support their positions. More important, the time necessary to conduct studies on this scale was longer than the duration of public interest in the issues being explored; the public climate in which the findings were received in the mid-1970s was a very different one from that which had launched them a few years earlier.

Whatever the factors—goals that are difficult to define, achievements that are difficult to measure, variables too complex to analyze quickly and comprehensively—there is a widespread impression that the effectiveness of social intervention has not been proved. Did the Job Corps make a difference? Or CETA? Or WIN? Or tougher drug laws? Or busing for desegregation? Or subsidized housing? People's answers are likely to depend on their personal beliefs, bolstered by whatever objective data support their views. To some extent such a situation is inevitable, but it is aggravated by the special problems associated with measuring achievement in human services.

Skepticism about Social Intervention

In addition to the inherent problems of objective evaluation, social programs in the United States face an additional obstacle to proving their effectiveness, that is, the lingering doubt among many Americans that social intervention is really needed. Though America is sometimes referred to as a welfare state, particularly in relation to its own past, this country has never gone as far as most Western European countries toward making private welfare and financial security a matter of primary public concern.

Broad social legislation, for instance, has generally come much later here than in Europe. Old-age pensions, begun in England in 1908, and unemployment insurance, initiated there in 1911, were not instituted in this country until 1935. Health insurance for the elderly, available in England since 1914, was finally passed in the United States in 1965. T. H. Marshall points out that in the Beveridge Report, which laid the framework for British welfare policies after World War II, social services are seen as the "centerpiece" of a good society.[45] It is hard to imagine such a statement being made in the United States, where the vision of a good society still turns more on individual achievement and self-actualization. In America, as we discussed earlier in this chapter, social intervention by the government is seen not as a part of daily life but as an emergency remedy to be applied only as absolutely necessary.

American support for the expansion of social welfare has tended to occur only when social conditions (interpreted, as we discussed in Chapter One, by articulate spokesmen inside and outside government) have seemed absolutely to require concerted action. Willingness to support social intervention has also been strengthened when it appeared that it could be accomplished without personal sacrifice or difficult policy choices. One of Franklin Roosevelt's most successful qualities, according to David Potter, was "his habit of assuming that benefits could be granted without costs being felt—an assumption rooted in his faith in the potentialities of the American economy."[46] Lyndon Johnson held the same view. "Can we move ahead with the Great Society programs and at the same time meet our needs for defense?" he asked in his 1966 Economic Report, "My confident answer is yes."[47]

In the years since 1970, however, growing economic constraints have made social welfare seem more like a zero-sum game.[48] In this "decade of decrement,"[49] traditional doubts about the validity of social expenditures have returned, often linked by our political leaders to a general distrust of government intervention in any field. Ronald Reagan has, perhaps, expounded this view most explicitly: "Government is not the solution to our problems. Government is the problem."[50] Such statements, echoing the comments of presidents Nixon, Ford, and Carter, have both sparked and reinforced growing public concern about the effectiveness of the social programs their tax dollars support. Traditional doubts about the effectiveness of government intervention in questions of social welfare have thus been aggravated by economic pressures and reinforced by recent political leaders.

The Search for Fiscal Accountability

When it is difficult to measure the results of social programs and when the public continues to hold doubts about their validity in any case (particularly as provided by government), it is not perhaps surprising that efficiency becomes the question at issue. Since effectiveness is difficult to prove, given the limitations of human service evaluation, and since even a technically solid proof might not dispel value-based doubts, efficiency becomes the one point on which disputants feel they can agree.

Yet trying to defend social welfare programs on the basis of their fiscal efficiency is a difficult undertaking. Costs do not exist in a vacuum, but as a means to achieving a desired end, which brings us again to questions of effectiveness and outcome. Human service managers find it hard to produce convincing data to justify program costs; this makes it easy for detractors to suggest that funds should be cut. If it is hard to show exactly what a given program has accomplished, it is even harder to show what will happen with 20 percent less money. Program managers sometimes lack data to reassure even themselves that program achievements are on target; it is more difficult yet to reassure consumers, elected officials, funding agencies, and the general public. Justifications are likely to fall back on measures of effort—how many visits, how many staff hours, how many admissions—both because the data are readily available and because they are satisfactorily measurable. But in the long run such figures do not reassure either those who offer them or those who receive them, and they are likely to initiate a spiraling debate on whether more visits per staff could be squeezed out, or more staff hours per week, or more admissions per clinic.

Gradually, the attention of both program managers and direct-line staff is diverted to monitoring what they know they can measure rather than what will truly let them and others know whether their efforts are succeeding.

At some level, the focus on efficiency becomes an issue of trust. Because social programs have trouble providing objective proof that their interventions are effective, they find themselves needing to justify each step along the way to prove that it was economic, efficient, and well managed. One of the most significant areas of distrust is the question of eligibility for service. Part of the reputation for "give-away programs" is based on the idea that many of those who benefit from social programs are not truly in need. It thus becomes part of every agency's task, as part of reassuring funding sources about the agency's efficiency and businesslike management, to ensure that no ineligible persons slip through its screening process. Verifying eligibility thus takes on an increasingly important role, since it becomes one of the ways that an agency attests to its overall management skills.

The monitoring of error rates—that is, of the extent to which benefits were paid incorrectly (and particularly overpaid)—has become another focus of tremendous attention. But it is important to understand that concerns about error rates go well beyond the rational analysis of expenditures. Their hold on people's interest is connected much more closely to the deep-seated wish that no assistance were necessary at all. "It is an interesting empirical question," observe Brodkin and Lipsky, "how much error rates would have to fall for public views of welfare administration to improve significantly."[51] A cost-benefit analysis of error-rate reduction suggests that it sometimes serves political and philosophical purposes as much as fiscal. A suit by the boards of education in New York, Cleveland, Milwaukee, Detroit, and Pittsburgh in 1983, for example, charged that a new Department of Agriculture policy for verifying eligibility in the school-lunch program could only bring in more than it cost to run if 32 percent of those checked were found to be ineligible; according to the cities, previous audits suggested error rates closer to 1 percent.[52] Young reports a pilot program in Los Angeles where error rates were reduced from 5.4 to 2.9 percent through expanded data-processing and other monitoring efforts, producing savings of $1 million; the only problem was that the pilot program itself cost $2 million.[53]

We see the result of the heavy emphasis on fiscal accountability at its clearest in the case of the stranded and fundless traveler who needs $20 for a bus ticket home. Before the traveler can receive $20 from a local welfare office, he may be detained for one or even two days while his eligibility is being confirmed. During this time, welfare may pay for his hotel room and devote staff time worth a considerable sum to verifying his eligibility, but the $20 cannot be provided until these procedures are complete.

It is appropriate that social programs should be accountable. The misfortune is that, because it is so difficult to prove objectively that the purposes for which the agency was created are being achieved, a less direct form of account-ability—proof of fiscal control—plays a disproportionately large role in judgments about the viability and effectiveness of social programs. Thus, the working principle that calls for accountability ends in exaggerated attention to efficiency and far too little to its original concern, that the programs under-taken should make a visible and significant difference.

In this atmosphere, the social welfare institution has become increasingly torn between the need to maximize service and the need to demonstrate fiscal accountability. Gradually, more and more attention is diverted from program-matic concerns. Divisions grow up between administrative and service staff, between funding sources and the agencies they support, between human ser-vices workers and the public, between clients who want benefits and staff who must ration them, and between competing groups of clients. The effect of this growing balkanization on both clients and care givers is the subject of the next chapter.

SUMMARY

This chapter presented four working principles of American social welfare—deficiency-oriented intervention, time-limited assistance, incrementalism, and accountability—and discussed them in terms of their impact on social pro-grams.

Deficiency-oriented intervention focuses social welfare efforts on chang-ing the client rather than changing social conditions. The recent histories of poverty programs and employment programs were explored as illustrations; in both areas, deficiency-oriented services were seen to predominate, starting in the Great Society years and continuing to the present. The tendency of such ap-proaches to encourage artificial divisions among client groups and among pro-viders was particularly noted.

Time-limited assistance is a principle that is easily traced to the American preference for defining social intervention as an exceptional and temporary oc-currence. The effects of this approach were traced in two examples: the denials of SSDI eligibility and the pattern of services developed for the homeless. Overdependence on time-limited approaches, it was suggested, tends to work against the creation of a stable system of care and to fragment efforts toward more fundamental reform.

Incrementalism stresses small-scale, step-by-step change rather than system-wide planning and development. While this principle offers practicality and political feasibility, it was shown to make shared planning more difficult, to divert human service staff from issues of broader reform, and to result in balkanized and uncoordinated organizational structures.

Accountability begins with the obligation to show that social welfare expenditures are justifiable. Because of the difficulty of evaluating human services and because of traditional doubts about the validity of government intervention in social welfare, attention narrows increasingly to questions of fiscal control. Gradually, this issue comes to dominate attention inside and outside the social welfare institution, to the detriment of the institution's more qualitative purposes.

NOTES

1. William Ryan, *Blaming the Victim* (New York: Vintage Books, 1976).
2. Economic Opportunity Act of 1964, *United States Statutes at Large*, vol. LXXVIII, sec. 2, p. 508.
3. Marc Miringoff, "OEO: The Formulation of Poverty Policy, A Study of the Relationship Between Social Analysis and Social Planning" (doctoral dissertation, University of Chicago, 1972), pp. 96–107.
4. Economic Opportunity Act, sec. 202(a) (2), p. 516.
5. Lawrence Friedman, "The Social and Political Context of the War on Poverty: An Overview," in Robert H. Haveman, ed., *A Decade of Federal Antipoverty Programs: Achievements, Failures and Lessons* (New York: Academic Press, 1977), p. 36.
6. "Democrats Lashed by Reagan Again," *New York Times*, Feb. 3, 1984, p. A10.
7. Sydney H. Schanberg, "Reagan's Homeless," *New York Times*, Feb. 4, 1984, p. 23.
8. "What Meese Said to the Reporters," *New York Times*, Dec. 15, 1983, p. 15.
9. "Reagan Seeks More Discipline in Schools," *New York Times*, Dec. 9, 1983, p. A26.
10. "Reagan Assails Great Society," *New York Times*, Dec. 4, 1983, p. A32.
11. Quoted in Frank J. Bruno, *Trends in Social Work 1874–1956* (New York: Columbia University Press, 1957), p. 72.
12. Rowland Evans, Jr. and Robert D. Novak, *Nixon in the White House: The Frustration of Power* (New York: Random House, 1971), p. 223.
13. Henry M. Levin, "A Decade of Policy Development in Improving Education and Training for Low-Income Populations," in Haveman, *A Decade of Federal Antipoverty Programs*, p. 175.
14. Richard P. Nathan, Robert F. Cook, and V. Lane Rawlins, *Public Service Employment: A Field Evaluation* (Washington, D.C.: Brookings Institution, 1981). For more information, see Thomas Meenaghan and Robert O. Washington, *Social Policy and Social Welfare: Structure and Applications* (New York: Free Press, 1980), pp. 162–181.
15. Harrison Donnelly, "Reagan-Backed Job Training Bill Approved," *Congressional Quarterly* 40 (40), Oct. 2, 1982, pp. 2427–2428; "New Job Program to Mark Big Shift," *New York Times*, Jan. 15, 1984, p. A19.
16. Gilbert Y. Steiner, "Reform Follows Reality: The Growth of Welfare," in Eli Ginzberg and Robert M. Solow, eds., *The Great Society: Lessons for the Future* (New York: Basic Books, 1974), p. 49. Similar comments from other public figures over the years appear on pp. 50–51 of this essay.
17. U.S. Department of Health and Human Services, *Recipient Characteristics Study* (Washington, D.C.: U.S. Government Printing Office, September 1980).
18. Evans and Novak, *Nixon in the White House*, p. 223.
19. S. G. and E. O. A. Checkland, eds., *The Poor Law Report of 1834* (London: Penguin Books, 1974), p. 335. The principle of less eligibility is also discussed in Karl de Schueinitz, *England's Road to Social Security: From the Statute of Laborers in 1349 to the Beveridge Report of 1942* (New York: A. S. Barnes & Company, 1943), pp. 114–127.
20. *Social Security Handbook* (Washington, D.C.: U.S. Government Printing Office, 1981), 7th ed., sec. 507 A, p. 81.
21. "Court Assails U.S. on Mentally Ill," *New York Times*, Aug. 29, 1984, p. A1.
22. "Benefits-Delay Said to Hurt Disabled," *New York Times*, Aug. 26, 1984, p. A42.

23. "Court Assails U.S. on Mentally Ill," *New York Times*, Aug. 29, 1984, p. B4.

24. "Congressional Panels Seek State Support for Disability Reform Bills," *Mental Health Reports* 8 (5), Feb. 29, 1984, p. 2.

25. The lower estimate was offered by the U.S. Department of Housing and Urban Development: "Homeless in U.S. Put at 250,000, Far Less Than Previous Estimates," *New York Times*, May 2, 1984, p. A1. The higher estimate is offered as an upper range in Kim Hopper, "Homelessness in America: An Overview" (presentation at the 1982 Annual Meeting of the American Public Health Association, Montreal, 1982).

26. Hopper, "Homelessness in America." See also *Private Lives/Public Spaces: Homeless Adults on the Streets of New York City* and *One Year Later: The Homeless Poor in New York City* (New York: Community Service Society, 1982).

27. John Coleman, "Diary of a Homeless Man," *New York Magazine*, Feb. 21, 1983, p. 30.

28. Mark Stern, "The Emergence of the Homeless as a Public Problem," *Social Services Review* 58 (2), June 1984, p. 295.

29. Alfred Kahn, *Theory and Practice of Social Planning* (New York: Russell Sage Foundation, 1969).

30. Charles E. Lindblom, "The Science of 'Muddling Through,' " *Public Administration Review* 19, Spring 1959, pp. 79–88. See also John C. Donovan, *The Policy Makers* (Indianapolis: Pegasus, 1970), pp. 100–117.

31. Lindblom, "Science of 'Muddling Through,' " p. 84. See also Etzioni's argument for a middle ground between Kahn and Lindblom in Amitai Etzioni, "Mixed-Scanning: A 'Third' Approach to Decision-Making," *Public Administration Review* 1, December 1967, pp. 385–392.

32. Joint Economic Committee of Congress, *Studies in Public Welfare, Paper No. 2* (Washington, D.C.: U.S. Government Printing Office, 1972).

33. Marc Bendick, Jr., and D. Lee Bawden, *Income-Conditioned Programs and Their Clients: A Research Agenda* (Washington, D.C.: Urban Institute, 1977), p. 35.

34. Ibid., p. 37.

35. Joseph A. Califano, Jr., *Governing America: An Insider's Report from the White House and the Cabinet* (New York: Simon and Schuster, 1981), p. 324.

36. American Public Welfare Association, *Public Welfare Directory*, 1983–1984.

37. Ibid.

38. Patricia Raber, "Health Care Alternatives for Aging Veterans," *Geriatrics* 38 (3), March 1983, pp. 39–44.

39. American Public Welfare Association, *Public Welfare Directory*.

40. Ibid.

41. Westinghouse Learning Corp., *The Impact of Head Start: An Evaluation of the Effects of Head Start on Children's Cognitive and Affective Development*, Ohio University Report to the Office of Economic Opportunity (Washington, D.C.: Clearinghouse for Federal Scientific and Technical Information, June 1969). (EDO36321)

42. Some of the problems involved in evaluating human services are discussed in Ellen Jane Hollingsworth, "Ten Years of Legal Services for the Poor," in Haveman, *A Decade of Federal Antipoverty Programs*, pp. 285–327; Walter Jones, "Can Evaluations Influence Programs? The Case of Compensatory Education," *Journal of Policy Analysis and Management* 2 (2), Winter 1983, pp. 174–184; Daniel Katz et al., *Bureaucratic Encounters: A Pilot Study in the Evaluation of Government Services* (Ann Arbor, Mich.: Survey Research Center, Institute for Social Research, 1975); Henry Aaron, *Politics and the Professors: The Great Society in Perspective* (Washington, D.C.: Brookings Institution, 1978); Sar Levitan, *The Great Society's Poor Law: A New Approach to Poverty* (Baltimore: Johns Hopkins Press, 1969); Clair Wilcox, *Toward Social Welfare: An Analysis of Programs and Proposals Attacking Poverty, Insecurity and Inequality of Opportunity* (Homewood, Ill.: Richard D. Irwin, Inc., 1969).

43. Joseph A. Pechman and P. Michael Timpane, eds., *Work Incentives and Income Guarantees: The New Jersey Negative Income Tax Experiment* (Washington, D.C.: Brookings Institution, 1975).

44. See U.S. Department of Housing and Urban Development, *Experimental Housing Allowance Program: Initial Observations* (Washington, D.C.: U.S. Government Printing Office, 1975); Raymond J. Struyk and Marc Bendick, Jr., *Housing Vouchers for the Poor: Lessons from a National Experiment* (Washington, D.C.: Urban Institute, 1981).

45. T. H. Marshall, "The Role of the Social Services."

46. David M. Potter, *People of Plenty* (Chicago: University of Chicago Press, 1954), pp. 120–121.

47. Quoted in Schanberg, "Reagan's Homeless," p. 23.

48. Lester M. Thurow, *The Zero-Sum Society*.

49. Yehezkel Dror, "Social Policy in Decrement: A Perspective of Governments," in *Conference on Social Policies in the 1980's: The Welfare State in Crisis* (Paris: Organization for Economic Cooperation and Development, 1981), pp. 260–274.

50. Ronald W. Reagan, Inaugural Address, Jan. 20, 1981, in *Public Papers: Ronald Reagan, 1981* (Washington, D.C.: U.S. Government Printing Office, 1982), p. 1.

51. Evelyn Brodkin and Michael Lipsky, "Quality Control in AFDC as an Administrative Strategy," *Social Services Review*, 57 (1), March 1983, p. 29.

52. "City Seeking to Block U.S. Rules on Verifying Income for School Lunch Aid," *New York Times*, Sept. 17, 1983, p. 29.

53. John Young, "Reflections on the Root Causes of Fraud, Abuse and Waste in Federal Social Programs," *Public Administration Review* 43 (2), March 1983, p. 366.

CHAPTER SEVEN

Clients, Staff, and the Social Welfare Institution

Jane Addams once wrote that "a man who takes the betterment of humanity for his aim and end, must also take the daily experiences of humanity for the constant correction of his process."[1] The purpose of this chapter is to address, as Jane Addams suggests, the daily experiences of those whose lives are most closely touched by the social welfare institution—the clients and the staff. The trends and tendencies we have described in earlier chapters, including the growing balkanization of agencies and programs, can be seen most clearly when we examine how social welfare programs affect individual lives. We will begin with the impact on clients and then consider how staff are affected.

CLIENTS IN A FRAGMENTED SYSTEM

William, age 47, was discharged [after 19 years in a state hospital] into a boarding home. . . . For the first 30 days, he did relatively well, but soon afterward he went off all medication, regressed, and left the boarding home for the streets of Philadelphia. He became floridly psychotic, unkempt, malodorous, out of touch with reality and extremely paranoid about being poisoned. His resulting physical problems included infestations of lice and maggots.

William could not be readmitted to the state hospital because he had been out of the hospital for more than 30 days. . . . To be readmitted . . . he first needed to spend 28 days in a private psychiatric hospital or psychiatric unit. No exceptions were made to that policy because the state hospital feared an inundation of patients being sent back from the 'community.' I made several attempts to have William admitted to the psychiatric unit of one of the private general hospitals, but each attempt was a failure. . . .

William was found dead behind a Philadelphia crisis center, his feet bitten by rats. I learned of his death when the county coroner phoned the state hospital volunteer who had worked with the patient for eight months before his discharge. The volunteer had tried to maintain contact with the patient, but was prevented by 'confidentiality' rules from locating him. When William died, the only means of identifying him was through a scrap of paper in his pocket containing the volunteer's name and phone number.[2]

William's story illustrates the individual suffering that can result from a dysfunctional social welfare system. A number of organizations were in place that might together have met his needs, and at least several caring individuals appear to have been involved, but he died because the barriers to service, combined with his own deep-seated problems, were more powerful than the efforts of those who wished to help.

Perhaps the most tragic aspect of William's story is that it is not an isolated event. In his story we see two ways in which the increasing balkanization of American social welfare makes it more difficult for clients to find the help they need. The first source of difficulty is the fact that clients' problems do not necessarily fit the categorizations imposed on them by social welfare's organizational structures. Second is the variety of confused and inconsistent messages that clients of the social welfare institution may receive. Let us explore each of these areas to assess how they affect clients' lives.

Administrative Categorization

For clients, one of the greatest difficulties associated with the growing balkanization of social welfare is the fact that human problems do not necessarily fit within the organizational boundaries often erected between different departments, different agencies, different levels of government, and different professional specialties. When a mental patient's changing service needs, for instance, take him or her from a state-run psychiatric facility to a privately owned group home, with aftercare services at a county-run clinic and periodic medical follow-up in a city hospital, the fragmentation of the service system can become a significant factor in his or her course of treatment. Patients' efforts to obtain care are too often complicated by questions of jurisdiction, eligibility and reimbursement structure—all related not to their psychiatric problems but to the organizational problems of the system that serves them.

Within individual agencies, other kinds of fragmentation exist. Communication may falter between professional disciplines, between outreach workers and those based in the office, between workers on different shifts, or between those who work with particular categories of clients. Whenever the client's needs cross these boundaries, there is a special necessity for consistency and coherence; too often these important elements are lacking.

Another form of fragmentation can be seen in the isolated focus on individual clients without sufficient regard for those who share their lives. Allison Murdach proposes a "political perspective in problem-solving."[3] Before you try to change a client, she advises, try to get an understanding of those whose lives intersect with the client, try to see what they gain or lose from the client's behavior, and what they will gain or lose if he or she changes. Murdach argues that a resolution of the problem, to last, must provide some payoff for both the client and the important people in the client's life; otherwise, either the client or they will undermine it as soon as the professional lets go. Learning to approach social welfare in this way requires a crossing of traditional boundaries, beyond single areas of specialization, beyond the concept of a single disabled patient. Looking at the family system, for example, as a dynamic structure in which the patient is only one element provides another way of moving away from fragmentation toward a more holistic and integrated approach to social welfare.

At each level of the social welfare institution the growing balkanization of social welfare has tended to make more difficult the kind of service continuity that most observers see as a desirable goal. More and more divisions arise, based on clients' disabilities, on funding source, on type of service, on service setting, on geography, on history. The alcoholic senior citizen must seek out one agency for his alcoholism and another for his age-related concerns; the family with an unemployed father and a retarded child must deal with two agencies and sometimes more; the teenage mother with a drug problem must do the same. In such a climate it is not uncommon to define clients' needs simply according to which agency saw them first. Thus, application to a child guidance clinic may mean that, whatever other problems a teenager presents, psychiatric change will be the central focus of treatment; yet if the same individual starts at a drug abuse center, or a school psychologist, or juvenile court, or a family therapy clinic, the whole approach to the client's situation may be formulated quite differently.

Looking at clients' lives instead of at fragmented social welfare structures opens new possibilities that seem more closely linked to the human realities of social problems. In New York State, for instance, a new program to combat teenage pregnancy focuses not only on birth control but on some of the other factors involved—broken homes, unemployment, and the search for dignity. "For an alarming number of the state's teenagers, being a parent has become part of growing up," says a spokesman. Many of these "children have children," he says, not by mistake, but because having a baby is a way of asserting their identity and independence.[4] Again, the complexity of human problems provides a powerful argument against rigid classification of service areas. The solution is not a program that provides only birth control or only counseling or only prenatal care, but one that responds to the diverse needs and motivations of the teenage mothers themselves.

We have discussed service fragmentation in terms of how it may interfere with providing the best care possible. Sometimes the outcome is much grimmer. Every year in every state there are cases where rigid divisions between agencies actually aggravate clients' troubles; some may even contribute to their deaths. In 1982 one such event was the death of Jerry Smith [pseudonym], a 21-year-old mildly retarded man. Mr. Smith appears to have been tortured over the course of two years by the three people with whom he lived; the three were ultimately convicted of the beatings that led to his death in March 1982. Subsequent investigation by the state Quality of Care Commission revealed the following:

> In August 1981, seven months before Mr. Smith's death, the county Department of Social Services received a report from a nearby county that two boys recently returned from foster care in Mr. Smith's home said he had been receiving regular severe abuse at the hands of his caretakers.
>
> After a home visit during which both Mr. Smith and his caretakers denied the charges, a DSS caseworker nevertheless concluded that the allegation might be true. A week later, she convened a meeting of representatives from her department, the local Mental Health Clinic, the Association for Retarded Children, and the Sheriff's Department.
>
> No minutes of the meeting were recorded, but the following facts emerged subsequently:

1. The Mental Health Clinic and the Sheriff's Department each thought the other had been assigned the lead role in following up the case; each waited for information from the other.
2. The DSS representative thought the clinic and sheriff representatives had agreed to make a home visit together.
3. In fact, the police took no further action on the case.

Mr. Smith did attend the Mental Health Clinic a few times, but no information from these visits was shared with DSS.

He was also examined during this period by at least two physicians, but neither was informed that abuse was suspected, so neither looked for evidence of it.

Although DSS policy requires that all Protective Services cases should be reviewed at monthly meetings, Mr. Smith's case was never discussed at such a meeting. One DSS staff member indicated later that she thought the case had been resolved, since it was never brought up again.

On March 6, 1982, Jerry Smith died, apparently as a result of a final beating by his caretakers.

After the caretakers were convicted of Mr. Smith's death, a Quality of Care Commission investigation was undertaken. Their summary of the case concluded: "Jerry Smith was the victim of abuse by caretakers who eventually caused his death. He was also the victim of the failure of a service system which was created by law to protect New York State's more vulnerable citizens."[5]

Clearly Jerry Smith's case was gravely complicated by his unwillingness to admit that he needed help; nevertheless, his story also presented a troubling picture of paralysis, noncommunication, and misunderstanding among agencies, even in the face of generally acknowledged suffering and danger.

Problems of this kind can affect clients in all parts of the social welfare institution. The unemployed alcoholic, the homeless mental patient, the ex-offender, the abused child, the patient with a medical emergency—each is likely to require the services of more than one provider. Clients' well-being, and sometimes even their lives, can be jeopardized if separations between agencies prevent vital communication and follow-up. In such cases, the fragmented structures erected for administrative clarity can exact a terrible cost, a cost that is paid most of all by the client.

Confusion and Inconsistency

If you were poor, you might have to fill out sixty separate forms to get help. . . . In Boston, a woman spent more than three hundred hours in one year completing assistance forms. In New York City, a single case-file drawn at random by federal investigators contained more than seven hundred application documents. In another city, an Army veteran made a 130-mile round trip to complete paperwork at a VA office—only to be told a few months later he would have to revisit the office personally to provide the same information for a different program. Elderly persons applying for Social Security benefits were required to submit information that had been in the agency's file for years, sometimes decades. In one case, a disabled woman was denied federal Medicaid payments for more than six months while welfare workers insisted that she provide a bank statement even though she had no bank account.[6]

This account by Haynes Johnson captures the repetitiveness and perversity that clients too often face. Much of the confusion is attributable to the growing balkanization of social welfare in recent years. As more and more individual programs have evolved—each conceived as a time-limited effort and many initiated with little thought for the related programs that already existed—there has necessarily been a tendency toward duplication and inconsistency. The growing emphasis on accountability has also played a part, placing increasing stress on screening, monitoring, and eligibility, so as to ensure that only those truly in need receive services. Guidelines have become tremendously complex. Young suggests that a significant portion of the inaccurate payments made by benefit programs are simply a result of the difficulty both staff and clients have in interpreting the intricate regulations.[7]

When staff are uncertain, the recent emphasis on tight controls leads them, as we noted earlier, to err on the side of conservatism. Clients, meanwhile, have such difficulty interpreting the guidelines that they frequently do not know if they have been denied services wrongfully. But some studies of the rate at which eligibility denials have been reversed following judicial review suggest that complicated guidelines are sometimes interpreted against clients' interests.[8] The difficulty is that the regulations are so difficult to interpret, the appeal process so demanding, and the time delays so great, that only those with unusual stamina, perseverance, and skill see the process through. For the rest, negotiating benefits can become a continuing process of requests, denials, delays, and further requests, in an atmosphere of wariness and uncertainty on both sides.

Confusion is not limited to questions of eligibility and benefit level. The American system of welfare is a tangled web of parallel and sometimes overlapping structures. The client is the one who must negotiate the tricky territory along the program boundaries, using the inconsistencies to his benefit if he is adroit but caught between conflicting forces if he is less skillful. AFDC, Medicaid, food stamps, day-care, school lunch, training grants, public housing—any or all of these may be available in different combinations depending on recipients' residence, employment status, family size, other income, and so forth. To maneuver one's way through the system, making the best arrangement at each point, takes an agility and sophistication that not many possess.

An example of the confusion that the fragmented welfare system produces is the policy on earned income. While the traditional rhetoric continues to exhort all recipients of public assistance to get jobs, the welfare payment structure provides little incentive for doing so. A few years ago, Henry Aaron noted that a mother of three in a well-paying state would do better earning $4,000 than $8,400, because at the latter level she would be off AFDC and thereupon lose both food stamps and Medicaid.[9] Although benefit levels vary in each state, the changes in the Omnibus Budget Reconciliation Act of 1981 make work even less attractive, since after the first four months every dollar earned is deducted from one's AFDC grant.

Barth observes that the inconsistencies in welfare programs are not there by accident; each represents a difficult trade-off that legislators found too costly (fiscally or politically) to resolve.[10] Work requirements are incorporated because of the concern for getting people off welfare, but workers lose nearly all their earnings because the public has been reluctant to see welfare benefits going to people who are earning too much money. AFDC mothers are encouraged to improve their earning power, but most are denied day-care if they are in training; families are urged to stay together, but eligibility for assistance is sharply reduced if the father or employed children are members of the household. These contradictions are understandable philosophically and historically from the point of view of those who make the laws, but they present a difficult double bind for those who must live by them.

Michael Lipsky argues that complicated procedures sometimes serve another purpose—that of rationing resources.[11] In an environment of shrinking funds and growing demand for services, he says, human service workers sometimes come to feel, correctly or incorrectly, that it is up to them to ration resources in whatever way they can. Hence, clients sometimes find informal and perhaps unacknowledged barriers placed in the way of service. These may include inconvenient office hours, inaccessible service locations, complicated application procedures, lack of information about available services, and appeal processes that involve many steps, long delays, and detailed paperwork. These "low-level marginal decisions, or nondecisions of low visibility," according to Lipsky, can limit service as significantly as funding cuts, without attracting nearly so much notice.

Of course, most of the confusion and inconsistency which clients encounter in their dealings with the social welfare institution is more inadvertent than the trade-offs Barth describes. Often, it is simply the result of multiple uncoordinated programs interacting in unanticipated ways.[12] The trend over the past decade toward more special-purpose programs, more decentralized policy structures, and a relatively unintegrated combination of public and private providers has increased the chances for unforeseen inconsistencies between the different elements of the social welfare institution.

Again, it is the client who must try to make sense of the increasingly balkanized system. Self-sufficiency is sometimes recommended, sometimes obstructed; family solidarity is sometimes praised, sometimes undermined; self-improvement is sometimes preached, sometimes blocked. Fundamentally, an institution that is clearly intended as a source of help sometimes seems to possess characteristics that make help very difficult to receive. In Edmund Rivera's story "Segundo and Magda," the central character applies for veterans' benefits and encounters a response that captures many of the problems we have described:

> When he went down for a hearing, a VA official told him that according to their records he had died back in 1963. He said he hadn't died in 1963, or any other year, as the official could see. "I'm standing right here, alive, as you can see," he said. "Do I look dead to you?"
>
> But he was told that his presence there was no proof that he was who he said he was. "We'll need your fingerprints," he was told. He gave them his fingerprints. He was told they would be sent to the FBI or whoever, and within a few weeks or so the VA would be in touch with him, let him know he was still alive.
>
> Whenever he calls to find out if he's been brought back to life in their records, they tell him his case is being processed, still pending. He calls them less often these days.[13]

The problems we have described that face clients in their dealings with the social welfare institution—the rigid administrative boundaries and the inconsistent or confusing procedures—are to a great extent attributable to the growing fragmentation of social welfare. At the same time, these conditions also tend to increase fragmentation by sharpening divisions between agencies, between clients and staff, and between groups of clients who see themselves as competing for a shrinking pool of resources. In this section we have explored the impact of these tendencies on social welfare clients; let us look next at what it means to work in the social welfare institution.

STAFF: THE STRESSFUL ROLE IN THE MIDDLE

> We had a lot of cases of teenagers who couldn't get along with their parents. . . . Usually I would place the child with foster parents, but it would only be temporary. The same problems would recur with the new family, who would be on the phone with the same complaints within a month or two. By that point the original home situation usually had calmed down, and the parents would take the child back.
>
> When I was just starting out, I would keep going back to visit the family and see how they were doing. I would arrange for followup counseling with a private agency and make sure the family actually went there. Later my attitude changed. If the family didn't call me, I didn't call them. It was easier to assume that everything was okay; if it wasn't, I didn't want to know about it. I hoped I'd never hear from them again. Unfortunately, things usually were not okay, and we'd have the family back in our laps some months later. I just hoped they would be assigned to someone else.[14]

In the voice of this demoralized staff member we hear themes that recur frequently in analyses of human service work: disappointed ideals, a sense of futility, and a growing effort to insulate oneself from the client's problems. Volumes have been written about the special emotional hazards of the helping professions; recent studies have explored occupational stress among nurses,[15] special education teachers,[16] alcoholism counselors,[17] day-care staff,[18] public welfare workers,[19] geriatric counselors,[20] mental health center staff,[21] mental retardation workers,[22] social workers,[23] guidance counselors,[24] ministers,[25] group-home parents,[26] school administrators,[27] mental hospital directors,[28] and a host of others.

Various names have been applied to the syndrome we are discussing: occupational stress, role strain, job tension, emotional exhaustion, role conflict, work-related stress, job dissatisfaction, burnout. Some terms appear to address genuinely different facets of the problem; others seem to be mere differences in nomenclature. But together they suggest a constellation of factors that are generally agreed to erode staff's sense of purpose and pride in relation to their work. For convenience, we will adopt as an operational definition the one offered by Edelwich in his book *Burnout: Stages of Disillusionment in the Helping Professions.* Burnout, Edelwich says, is "the progressive loss of idealism, energy and purpose experienced by people in the helping professions as a result of the conditions of their work."[29]

There is something, it seems clear, about work in the human services that wears down many who undertake it. Some of the factors involved have existed for decades, although in each decade some staff have found these stresses offset by the personal and professional satisfactions that the work brought as well. Our task, however, is to look specifically at the present day and assess how the characteristics of the social welfare institution as it is now influence staff's feeling about their work. We will examine it from three perspectives: goals, work roles, and rewards.

Unfulfilled Goals

Erving Goffman has captured in one sentence the dilemma faced by human services staff with regard to their agencies' goals: "The contradiction between what the institution does and what its officials must say it does forms the basic context of the staff's daily activity."[30] The gap between goals and reality has always been a problem for those who work in the human services. To some extent, the extravagance of expectations flows from the optimism and high aspirations with which many enter the field. Cherniss, for example, describes the gradual discouragement of a woman working in a legal services center:

> In some respects, poverty law was what Margaret had hoped it would be. When she was a law student, she was concerned about taking a job in which she would be compelled to do things she felt were morally wrong. A strong career need was to find work in which it would be possible to maintain her moral integrity. . . .
> However, in other respects, poverty law work in a neighborhood legal service agency proved to be a bitter disappointment for Margaret. . . . At one point, she

described her work as a "big band-aid" and said she was frustrated that it did not lead to "real" change. . . . Her work seemed to lack real meaning because it did not challenge legal and social institutions. Instead, the basic legal and social practices remained unquestioned while she spent days on the phone finding out why a client's Social Security check had been delayed.[31]

Part of Margaret's disillusion, we might conclude, can be traced to the high ideals with which she began her career. Perhaps any daily routine would have seemed disappointing compared to her vision of serving social justice. Yet even more down-to-earth workers have been troubled by the contrast between possibility and actuality in human services.

Trends over the past decade have exacerbated these stresses, as the aspects of agency functioning that give staff the most trouble have been reinforced and intensified. The increasing commitment to time-limited assistance and incremental planning make it very difficult for agencies—or for the social welfare institution as a whole—to provide more than stop-gap assistance. Yet at the same time social programs are being criticized with growing stridence for failing to resolve problems that have plagued society for many years: Why haven't the schools taught students to read? Why haven't the mental hospitals prepared their patients better for community life? Why haven't welfare workers got their clients back to work?

At upper levels of legislation or management, ambitious standards of program accomplishment may still be set; but ultimately hard decisions must be made, limited resources allocated, and inherent contradictions faced. This task, most frequently, falls to those who carry the programs out. "You should see the 'statements of mission' and 'guidelines' we have in our catalogues," says a college counselor:

> Our original statement of purpose included community services that the legislature never appropriated a penny for. A couple of years ago there was a great ferment in our area. The college administration wrote up guidelines, duly enacted by the board of trustees, that mandated funding and full recognition by the college. A visitor from outer space might expect to see some correlation between these directives and the actuality. But that's all the guidelines really do; they make the program look good to someone who's reading the catalogue.[32]

Michael Lipsky identifies the same pattern in a wide range of agencies. Everywhere, he says, the inconsistencies between expectation and funding level, between goal and reality, are passed on down the line, often until they reach the staff who work directly with clients. Somehow these workers must find a way of living with the contradictions that those above them on the ladder have not resolved. Lower-level staff, says Lipsky,

> often spend their work lives in a corrupted world of service. They believe themselves to be doing the best they can under adverse circumstances, and they

develop techniques to salvage service and decision-making values within the limits imposed upon them by the structure of the work. They develop conceptions of their work and of their clients that narrow the gap between their personal and work limitations and the service ideal. These work practices and orientations are maintained even while they contribute to the perversion of the service ideal or put the worker in the position of manipulating citizens on behalf of the agencies for which citizens seek help.[33]

There is a considerable literature on the subject of organizational goals and how "official" goals, such as providing quality care, can be overshadowed or displaced by such "operational" goals as maintaining jobs, maximizing revenues, or protecting individuals' careers.[34] Our concern here is not with the fact that goal displacement occurs, but with its impact on the workers involved. Staff are generally portrayed as the *actors* in goal displacement, the ones who distort the official goals of the organization for purposes of survival or profit; here we see that staff are also frequently the *victims*, paying in stress, disillusion, and burnout for the discrepancy between what the public (and they themselves) would like to see accomplished and what they are actually able to do.

Role Constriction

One of the ways in which human services staff make their peace with the discrepancy between theoretical goals and less satisfying reality is through the way they define their work roles. Whether they are managers, trained professionals, or line staff, their problem is the same: to define their work in a way that leaves some possibility of success. This natural tendency is by no means a new phenomenon, but neither is it unaffected by trends in the social welfare institution. One of the tasks of any social system is to reinforce the constructive inclinations of staff and to block or discourage those inclinations that will be dysfunctional. Thus, even though it is an understandable human tendency to limit one's vulnerability through staking out a particular sphere of control, a system like the social welfare institution can make it easier or more difficult to act on such inclinations. At the present time, the focus on case-by-case approaches, the disinterest in systematic reform, the expectation of quick and not too costly results, all tend to reinforce staff's natural tendency to interpret their roles as narrowly as possible.

Administrators.   For program administrators, one avenue of retreat from vulnerability is into the minutiae of daily administration. This can be viewed in terms of Miringoff's distinction between service management and maintenance management. According to Miringoff, service management is addressed to the "overall quality of the organization's service product," whereas maintenance management is concerned with "efficiency in the use of resources and with survival."[35] Although both are necessary, the most productive results occur, Miringoff shows, when service management is emphasized. But the temptations not to do so are powerful, since service management is more complex, more difficult to define, and much more dependent on collaborative efforts. Being human, managers often prefer to concentrate on the turf that is most clearly theirs—simple maintenance. Thus, even high-level managers will sometimes take personal responsibility for relatively minor aspects of the agency's daily operations—space allocation, details of hiring and promotion, logistical arrangements—thus unconsciously ensuring that there is no time left for the knottier problems of overall program direction and outcome.

In recent years the continuing struggle to obtain, allocate, and justify scarce resources has reinforced managers' inclination to shy away from more qualitative efforts. Increasingly, program administrators have tended to focus their energies on justifying the demand for existing services rather than taking a fresh look at how their resources might be combined with others to achieve better outcomes. Such objectivity never comes easily; today's climate makes it still more difficult. "I was disdainful of bureaucrats," says a project coordinator in a youth program:

> I said I could replace a bureaucrat and conduct a program in relationship to people, not figures. I doubt seriously if three years from now I'll be involved in public administration. One reason is each day I find myself more and more like unto the people I wanted to replace.[36]

Managers' concentration on obtaining and conserving resources has tended to sharpen the natural differences in orientation between administrators and service providers. Service staff sometimes come to feel that, in the eyes of management, the week with the greatest number of reimbursable visits is the most productive week, regardless of what takes place during the interactions. The result is one more form of balkanization, in which important elements of the social welfare institution are increasingly isolated from each other and in which rigid distinctions between the two groups obscure their mutually dependent roles in addressing social problems.

Professionals. As managers become caught in the more mechanical roles prescribed by maintenance management, other traps exist for service-giving professionals. Troubled by the discrepancy between goals (both the agency's and their own) and what can actually be achieved, caught between the expectations of management and of clients, these professionals begin to look for ways to make their work situation less stressful.

One way, which recent trends have strongly reinforced, is to accept the premise that social problems originate primarily because of something in the client. Under this principle, professionals can still do their best to improve matters, but it is assumed from the beginning that the client is the principal source of difficulty; if success is not achieved, the failure can be at least partially explained by the client's own failings.

The focus on client's failings often intensifies when staff feel discouraged or unappreciated. This description of an inner-city chemistry teacher interviewed periodically during his first year of teaching suggests how professionals can react as unachieved goals and other stresses begin to weigh upon them:

> He gradually abandoned what seemed to him to be the perfectionist ideal of "reaching" every student. He came to believe that student performance depended more on the student's "given ability" and less on the teacher. He also came to believe that, no matter what a teacher did, some students would not like the class and would not want to work. Initially, he had attempted to reach *all* of his students, but by the followup interview, he minimized his sense of personal responsibility for student interest, ability, performance.[37]

Consistent with the emphasis on client deficits is the stress on professional specialization. When work in the social welfare institution is particularly stressful—because of limited resources, unrealistic expectations, and public criticism—the emphasis on specialization can be expected to increase, since it offers the professional a way of exerting some control over the environment within which he functions.

When specialization is exaggerated, professionals may begin to see clients' needs entirely in terms of what they themselves are trained and certified to offer. Erik Erikson gives us one example of this tendency, based on his review of the psychiatric treatment provided to returning veterans after World War II. Although these patients, according to Erikson, were frequently responding to real changes in American society and in America's world role, the psychiatrists identified each one as needing psychotherapy:

> This emphasis on individual treatment even where the patient seemed anything but introspective and verbal can be seen as a widespread resistance against the awareness of a failure of social mechanisms under radically changing historical determinants. . . . The psychiatrist, in disregarding the contributions of such developments to neurotic discomfort, is apt not only to miss much of the specific dynamics in contemporary life cycles; he is apt also to deflect individual energy from the collective tasks at hand.[38]

The same trap awaits other professionals if their perceptions of clients' needs are limited too sharply by their own special training and competencies.

But it is pointless to criticize deficit-oriented intervention or professional specialization for the limits they impose on staff's perceptions, when that is precisely their appeal: They impose structure on an unwieldy mass of human problems. Indeed, many other boundary-defining behaviors for which human service professionals are criticized spring from the same motivation. The school principal who denies the existence of any drug problems among his students, the nutrition center that avoids the question of how its clients get through the weekend, the vocational counselor who focuses his energies on the most promising students—all these individuals are making an understandable human response to a difficult situation. They feel accountable for producing successful results, and they wish to define the problems they confront in a way which gives them some hope of success.

Line staff.   Perhaps no members of the social welfare institution are faced with so ambiguous a role as those who deal most directly with clients—the group Michael Lipsky calls "street-level bureaucrats":[39] the caseworker, the hospital attendant, the group-home parent, the teacher, the home health aide, the child-care worker. Unprotected by administrative responsibilities or professional specialization, these workers are most vulnerable to the contradictions of the overall system. Many feel they are caught in the middle of a tug-of-war, not sure whether they are the client's advocate with the agency or the agency's advocate with the client. A "patient's representative" in a general hospital describes her job:

> I'm the buffer between the patient and the collection department. . . . We visit our patients as often as we can, so they get to know us as their representative. "Are you comfortable?" "Are you satisfied with your food?" Then, when he gets to know me—"I know your account is going to be a problem . . ." I'm not looking for money, but if the patient doesn't ask such questions, I mention it. I sort of joke with 'em and then lay it out and sock it to 'em. . . .
>
> I don't get into many arguments with patients. They're more or less at my mercy. They can't say too much. Once you're in the hospital and you owe me money, if I talk to you in a sympathetic way, you're not gonna get too sarcastic about it. If you owe me money, I can't ignore that fact. You may be sick and dying and I like you a lot and you make me cry and all that. I still got to go in and talk to you about your bill. That's what's hard.[40]

Many human service jobs are less patently based on agency needs than that of the patients' representative quoted above, but role ambiguity is common. The caseworker, for instance, who is responsible both for providing welfare benefits and for denying them, is in a difficult middle-ground position. It is not surprising that people in these jobs sometimes feel like clients' friends, and sometimes like policemen. In earlier years, nearly every aspect of a welfare recipient's life was open to inspection by caseworkers, as this sample from an early manual of the Louisiana Department of Public Welfare attests:

> The fact that a mother has dates with a man does not in itself establish that a nonlegal marital union exists. However, the worker shall be alert to and follow up on clues which indicate that the relationship is more than that of dating or courtship. . . . When there is indication that the relationship may be more than that of normal courtship this should be discussed with the client, who should be asked for a true and full account concerning the length of time she has been seeing the man in question, when she usually sees him, the frequency of their dates and where they go.[41]

Interest in clients' love lives may have diminished, but "man-in-the-house" guidelines still are followed to determine whether women receiving public assistance are living with men who might be expected to contribute to their support. These guidelines came to public notice, for instance, in the spring of 1984 when presidential candidate Jesse Jackson spent the night with a welfare family in New York City: The publicity surrounding his visit attracted the attention of the local welfare office, which noted the presence of the father in the newspaper pictures and immediately sent a worker to review the family's welfare eligibility.[42]

The stress for the worker, of course, is that his loyalties frequently pull him in both directions. As an agent of the program, he is accountable for allocating its resources with care. As the person who works most closely with the clients, he is constantly aware of when the agency's efforts fall short in meeting clients' needs. The dramatic reduction of available funds in recent years has only aggravated this problem.

Earlier in this chapter, we cited Lipsky's analysis of how services are denied to clients through "bureaucratic disentitlement," including such measures as limited office hours, complicated application procedures, and rigid interpretations of regulations.[43] When we discussed such approaches from the point of view of the client, we focused on the client's feelings of frustration and rejection. Now, looking at the same behavior from the worker's point of view, we understand that these measures are instituted most of all as a way of creating an imperfect but at least bearable balance between agency purposes and available resources.

Frances Perkins observed once that "Man must so administer the laws of men that the laws of God will have a chance to operate, too."[44] In recent years, many human service workers have found that combination almost impossible to achieve.

Lack of Rewards and Recognition

Like employees everywhere, human service staff need rewards and recognition to sustain their efforts. The rewards need not be monetary, and the recognition need not be formal; what is necessary is some systematic reassurance that staff's contributions are valued.

The ideal source of rewards is the client. Knowledge that one has made a real difference in someone's life has always been one of human services' most powerful satisfactions. But human service agencies deal in trouble, and there are always more problems than solutions. People working in these fields are society's surrogates for handling all the difficulties that could not be resolved elsewhere: poverty, age, sickness, disability, insanity, unemployment, hunger, homelessness, bereavement, abuse, neglect. Problems are not always soluble; clients are not always grateful; the cured get sick again. However altruistic their motivation, human service staff cannot derive all the rewards they need from client outcome.

Beyond client response, the worker looks to the organization for support. Organizational support, however, is not always well developed in the human services; observers frequently comment that human services organizations sometimes do surprisingly little to foster the health, education, or welfare of their employees. In the previous section we discussed some of the pressures, particularly in recent years, that have led managers to focus exclusively on maintenance and accountability. This focus then makes less likely the kind of support and qualitative feedback that lower-level staff need. Instead, management tends to stress the objective measures that external agencies request (such as test scores, discharge rates, placement rates, error rates, absenteeism, unit costs, and so forth). Such measures frequently produce useful information, but they leave staff feeling that the most difficult, interesting, and significant part of their work has gone unrecognized.

Workers know, for example, that two job placements from an employment program that appear statistically identical on a chart may in fact represent tremendously different investments of time and personal energy. Similarly, they know that they can spend days working to resolve some organizational dysfunction, work that may not be reflected immediately or at all in increased numbers but that may make a fundamental difference to clients' lives. If, for example, a group of clients need to attend a sheltered workshop, the easiest way of arranging it may be to schedule a regular van pick-up. Under some circumstances, however, a better approach might be to work with a local bus company to arrange that public bus routes include the workshop. This might involve repeated meetings, scheduling problems, and perhaps discussions with other agencies that have similar needs. Yet the outcome might go much further toward integrating the clients in the community and encouraging their independence.

Current trends in the social welfare institution tend to discourage this kind of effort, stressing instead a deficit-oriented client-specific approach that maximizes quantifiable services and minimizes the need for system-level change. Workers may feel some of the same inclinations themselves; only with continuing institutional support are they likely to tackle the broader questions.

Beyond the client and beyond the organization lies another potential source of reward or recognition—the public. The past ten years have not been a good period for the social welfare institution in terms of public approval. While the origins of these negative feelings are complex and in many ways unrelated to those who work in the area of social welfare, workers in the field have come in for their share of blame. Advocacy on behalf of social programs by human services staff has often been interpreted as camouflaged job protection; social programs have been widely criticized for wasteful management and careless verification procedures; and there has been a generally expressed dissatisfaction with actual program outcomes—students who cannot read, welfare mothers still unemployed, discharged mental patients roaming the streets.

Workers themselves share many of these concerns, but the intensity of the public criticism makes them doubt whether it is even worthwhile to keep struggling. A teacher says:

> I walked into a supermarket the other day and the boy who was checking out my groceries said "Hello, Mrs. _____" with such love. . . . He's 18 years old, and they remember me. A lot of kids that I meet years later have wonderful memories. . . . Then, all of a sudden, people say, "You're no good." Who is right? Maybe I'm really not that good. Maybe I should never have gone into teaching.[45]

A survey of Connecticut social workers in 1980 found that nearly half would *not* choose the field again if they had it to do over; further analysis showed that most who would not be social workers again enjoyed the work and, although they were not satisfied with their pay, were no more dissatisfied than other respondents who said they *would* choose social work again. The distinguishing variable, it turned out, was respondents' perception of the prestige of social work; three-quarters of those who felt its prestige was "low" or "very low" were people who said they would not choose social work again.[46]

The same reactions recur throughout the human services field. Troubled already by their own awareness of unachieved goals and unresolved problems, staff is particularly sensitive to public criticism. Working in a field where the technology is often inexact, social welfare staff are all the more vulnerable to outside comments that confirm their doubts. The growing tendency to believe that the social welfare institution exists primarily to provide emergency help as inexpensively as possible for as brief a period as possible further undercuts workers' sense of prestige and permanency. Overall, neither public response nor client outcome nor organizational support has completely succeeded in providing human services workers with a significant level of recognition and reward.

Unfulfilled goals, constricted work roles, and lack of recognition—these are problems that many human service staff encounter in their work. The increasing balkanization of the social welfare institution in recent years has tended to aggravate these difficulties; its stress on the separateness of individual clients, different agencies, and different levels of government has limited the effectiveness of the institution and therefore limited the satisfactions of work within it. Simultaneously, staff's understandable responses to the balkanization of social welfare have tended to reinforce the very trends that cause them difficulty.

This concludes our analysis of the dynamics of social welfare, which we reviewed at the conceptual level in Chapter Five, at the operational level in Chapter Six, and at the level of clients and staff in Chapter Seven. In the next section, Part III, we will consider the implications of these trends for future policy making and explore what actions could be taken to build on the social welfare institution's present strengths while resolving some of the dysfunctions we have identified in Part II.

SUMMARY

In this chapter we have moved from analyzing the social welfare institution in terms of systems and programs to a consideration of how it affects the individual lives it touches—those of clients and staff.

Clients of the social welfare institution are impacted, first, by the rigid boundaries between agencies, between professions, and between governmental levels; these boundaries often seem designed more for administrative convenience than to optimize service capability. A second source of difficulty is the combination of elaborate procedures and contradictory guidelines, which interfere with clients' ability to receive help. In these ways, the growing balkanization of the social welfare institution has made it more difficult for clients to receive the human services they need.

Staff, meanwhile, are often caught in a conflict between the problems described above and the high expectations that both the public and they themselves hold for social programs. Reacting to the discrepancy, staff are likely to find ways of insulating themselves: managers through preoccupation with issues of accountability and professionals through informal and sometimes unacknowledged rationing of service. These responses further undermine the cohesion and effectiveness of the social welfare institution, making it less able to fulfill the expectations of clients, staff, and the broader society.

NOTES

1. Jane Addams, *Democracy and Social Ethics* (Cambridge, Mass.: Harvard University Press, 1964), p. 176.
2. Frank R. Lipton, Albert Sabatini, and Steven E. Katz, "Down and Out in the City: The Homeless Mentally Ill," *Hospital & Community Psychiatry* 34 (9), September 1983, p. 817.
3. Allison D. Murdach, "A Political Perspective in Problem Solving," *Social Work* 27 (5), September 1982, pp. 417-421. Similar emphases on viewing the client in the context of the family are found in G. Bateson et al., "Toward a Therapy of Schizophrenia," *Behavioral Sciences* 1, pp. 251-264; M. Bowen, "The Use of Family Theory in Clinical Practice," *Comprehensive Psychiatry* 7, pp. 345-374; I. Boszormenyi-Nagy and J. L. Framo, eds., *Intensive Family Therapy* (New York: Hoeber, 1965); J. Haley, *Strategies of Psychotherapy* (New York: Grune and Stratton, 1963); S. L. Halleck, "Family Therapy and Social Change," *Social Casework* 57, pp. 483-493; R. B. Stuart, "Behavioral Contracting with the Families of Delinquents," *Journal of Behavior Therapy and Experimental Psychiatry* 2, pp. 1-11; L. C. Wynne et al., "Pseudo-mutuality in the Family Relations of Schizophrenics," *Psychiatry* 21, pp. 205-220.
4. "Cuomo Offers Program on Teen-Age Pregnancy," *New York Times*, Apr. 6, 1984, p. B2.

5. New York State Commission on Quality of Care for the Mentally Disabled and the Mental Hygiene Medical Review Board, *In the Matter of Jerry Smith: A Mentally Retarded Resident of Fulton County*, May 1984, p. xvi.

6. Haynes Johnson, *In the Absence of Power: Governing America* (New York: Viking Press, 1980), p. 50.

7. John Young, "Reflections on the Root Causes of Fraud, Abuse and Waste in Federal Social Programs," *Public Administration Review* 43 (2), March 1983, pp. 362–369.

8. See, for example, Michael Lipsky, "Bureaucratic Disentitlement in Social Welfare Programs," *Social Service Review* 58 (1), March 1984, p. 13, regarding reversal rates in Massachusetts, and "SSA Orders States to Cut Disability Benefits," *Mental Health Reports* 8 (3), Feb. 1, 1984, p. 2, for description of high rates of reversals on cases where disability benefits were cut off and then appealed.

9. Henry Aaron, *Why Is Welfare so Hard to Reform? A Staff Paper* (Washington, D.C.: Brookings Institution, 1973), p. 33.

10. Michael C. Barth, George J. Carcagno, and John L. Palmer, *Toward an Effective Income Support System: Problems, Prospects and Choices* (Madison, Wis.: Institute for Research on Poverty, University of Wisconsin, 1974), p. 125.

11. Lipsky, "Bureaucratic Disentitlement," p. 20. This subject is discussed further in Lipsky, *Street-Level Bureaucracy* (New York: Russell Sage Foundation, 1980); and Jeffrey Manditch Prottas, "The Cost of Free Services," *Public Administration Review* 41 (5), September 1981, pp. 526–534.

12. See, for example, Gordon H. Lewis, "The Day Care Tangle: Unexpected Outcomes when Programs Interact," *Journal of Policy Management and Analysis* 2 (4), Summer 1983, pp. 531–547.

13. Edward Rivera, "Segundo and Magda," *Public Welfare* 42 (2), 1984, p. 21.

14. Jerry Edelwich, *Burn-Out: Stages of Disillusionment in the Helping Professions* (New York: Human Sciences Press, 1980), p. 187.

15. Thomas S. Bateman and Stephen Strasser, "A Cross-Lagged Regression Test of the Relation Between Job Tension and Employee Satisfaction," *Journal of Applied Psychology* 68 (3), August 1983, pp. 439–445; I. Fawzy, et al., "Preventing Nursing Burnout: A Challenge for Liaison Psychiatry," *General Hospital Psychiatry* 5 (2), July 1983, pp. 141–149; Marlene Kramer, *Reality Shock: Why Nurses Leave Nursing* (St. Louis: C. V. Mosby Company, 1984).

16. Michael J. Fimian and Theresa M. Santoro, "Sources and Manifestations of Occupational Stress as Reported by Full-Time Special Education Teachers," *Exceptional Children* 49 (6), April 1983, pp. 543–549.

17. B. P. Sarata, "Burnout Workshops for the Alcohol Counselor," *Journal of Drug and Alcohol Education* 28 (3) Spring 1983, pp. 34–46.

18. Victoria J. Dimidjian, "Understanding and Combatting Stress in Family Day Care," *Journal of Child Care* 1 (2), September 1982, pp. 47–58.

19. Wendy Ruth Sherman and Stanley Wenocur, "Empowering Public Welfare Workers through Mutual Support," *Social Work* 28 (5), September-October 1983, pp. 375–379.

20. Susan Quattrochi-Tubin, John W. Jones, and Virginia Breedlove, "The Burnout Syndrome in Geriatric Counselors and Service Workers," *Activities, Adaptation and Aging* 3 (1), Fall 1982, pp. 65–76.

21. Cynthia B. Freier, "Study of Job Stress among Staff of Maimonedes Community Mental Health Center," *Journal of Preventive Psychiatry* 1 (3), 1982, pp. 349–351.

22. John K. Stout and John H. Williams, "Comparisons of Two Measures of Burnout," *Psychological Reports* 53 (1), August 1983, pp. 283–289.

23. Srinika Jayaratne, Tony Tripodi, and Wayne A. Chess, "Perceptions of Emotional Support, Stress and Strain by Male and Female Social Workers," *Social Work Research and Abstracts* 19 (2), Summer 1983, pp. 19–27.

24. Susan J. Sears and Sally L. Navin, "Stressors in School Counselors," *Education* 103 (4), Summer 1983, pp. 333–337. See also Douglas Thompson and Stephen Powers, "Correlates of Role Conflict and Role Ambiguity among Secondary School Counselors," *Psychological Reports* 52 (1), February 1983, pp. 239–242.

25. Helen Doohan, "Burnout: A Critical Issue for the 1980's," *Journal of Religion and Health* 21 (4), Winter 1982, pp. 352–358.

26. B. P. Sarata and Jo Ann Behrman, "Group Home Parenting: An Examination of the Role," *Community Mental Health Journal* 18 (4), Winter 1982, pp. 274–285.

27. Jack Brimm, "What Stresses School Administrators," *Theory into Practice* 22 (1), Winter 1983, pp. 64–69.

28. Diane M. Pinchoff and Mahmud Mirza, "The Changing Role of the State Hospital Director: Restructuring the Top Management Team," *Administration in Mental Health*, Winter 1982, pp. 92–103.

29. Edelwich, *Burn-Out*, p. 14. See also Naomi Gottlieb, *The Welfare Bind* (New York: Columbia University Press, 1974), pp. 26–28.

30. Erving Goffman, *Asylums* (Garden City, N.Y.: Doubleday & Company, 1961), p. 74.

31. Cary Cherniss, *Professional Burnout in Human Service Organizations* (New York: Praeger Publishers, 1980), pp. 138–139.

32. Edelwich, *Burn-Out*, p. 119.

33. Lipsky, *Street-Level Bureaucracy*, p. xiii. See also Lipsky, "The Welfare State as Workplace," *Public Welfare* 39 (3), Summer 1981, pp. 22–27.

34. See, for instance, Charles Perrow, "An Analysis of Goals in Complex Organizations," *American Sociological Review* 26 (6), 1961, pp. 854–866; Robert Michels, *Political Parties* (New York: Dover Press, 1969); James Thompson and William McEwan, "Organizational Goals and Environment: Goal Setting as an Interactive Process," *American Sociological Review* 23 (1), February 1958, pp. 23–31; Donald Cressey, "Achievement of an Unstated Organizational Goal," *Pacific Sociological Review* 1 (2), pp. 43–49.

35. Marc L. Miringoff, *Management in Human Service Organizations* (New York: Macmillan Publishing Co., 1980), pp. 97–98.

36. Studs Terkel, *Working* (New York: Pantheon Books, 1974), p. 341.

37. Cherniss, *Professional Burnout*, p. 151.

38. Erik Erikson, *Identity: Youth and Crisis* (New York: W. W. Norton & Company, 1968), p. 68.

39. Lipsky, *Street-Level Bureaucracy*.

40. Terkel, *Working*, pp. 498, 500.

41. Manual of the Louisiana Department of Public Welfare, sec. 2–742, J (mimeographed).

42. "Jackson Spends a Night in the South Bronx," *New York Times*, Mar. 31, 1984, p. A28.

43. Lipsky, "Bureaucratic Disentitlement," pp. 20–32.

44. George Martin, *Madame Secretary: Frances Perkins* (Boston: Houghton Mifflin Company, 1976), p. 282.

45. Fred Hechinger, "Teachers Talk about Powerlessness and Frustration," *New York Times*, Feb. 14, 1984, p. C8.

46. Laura Reiter, "Professional Morale and Social Work Training: A Study," *Clinical Social Work Journal* 8 (3), 1980, pp. 198–205.

CHAPTER EIGHT

Directions for Social Welfare: Redressing the Balance

In the opening pages of this book we suggested that the way the social welfare institution is presently organized and implemented has been a contributing factor to its diminishing public support in recent years. In Parts I and II we explored this idea further, analyzing three principal elements of the institution—values, technology, and structure—and showing how recent trends in these elements have interacted to create the social welfare institution we see today. We argued that recent tilts toward more traditional values, more rehabilitative technologies, and more decentralized structures have tended to balkanize the institution, reducing its ability to achieve the goals that those who work in it, are served by it, and support it all share.

An institution already under attack, by the public in general and by political leaders in particular, is obviously at an even greater disadvantage if its own philosophical, technical, and structural characteristics are diminishing its cohesion and effectiveness. Given, therefore, the combination of external and internal factors at work, there are necessarily some who will argue that the social welfare institution no longer has a place in American society, or if it does, its role should be greatly diminished. Such an argument maintains that the very existence of a social welfare institution is questionable. In an era when individualism and self-reliance are highly valued, it is possible to maintain that individual welfare is a matter that for the most part concerns only those involved, not the wider society and that social well-being consists of freeing individuals to pursue their own interests rather than of taking proactive steps for the general good.

As we noted in the Preface, our values run counter to this perspective. However, it is necessary that it be considered before proceeding to a presentation of the ways in which social welfare should be changed. Any argument against this view is fundamentally one of value. We cannot prove empirically that social welfare is a "good thing." The explanation can, however, be buttressed and illuminated by the presentation of certain concepts. We would argue, first, that social welfare as a public institution can contribute to society in ways that individual efforts cannot, helping to reduce human deprivation, isolation, and detachment. Also, we would argue that the institution tends to increase society's positive energy and degree of civilization. We are not maintaining that social welfare to date has been fully successful in achieving these goals; we are, rather, saying that it has the capacity and potential to do so. What is it, then, that constitutes this degree of civilization and energy in society? Let us examine the writings of some of those who, working in different fields, have considered this question.

SOCIAL WELFARE AND SOCIETY

Civilization, Synergy, and I-Thou

Sigmund Freud in his essay "Civilization and Its Discontents" distinguished between two kinds of energy that he felt existed in both individuals and societies. One he termed Eros; the other he called Thanatos, the death instinct. Eros represented to Freud not simply love, but a more fundamental life-giving energy: "the instinct and the desire to transgress the individual boundary . . . and to join it into an ever larger unit." Freud described Thanatos as "another, contrary, instinct seeking to dissolve those units and to bring them back to their primeval, inorganic state." That is to say, Freud identified both Eros, an instinct for life, and Thanatos, a conflicting instinct for death. "The phenomenon of life can be explained from the mutually opposing action of these two instincts."

Civilization, to Freud, is a process

> in the service of Eros, whose purpose is to combine single human individuals, and after that families, then races, peoples and nations, into one great unity, the unity of mankind. . . . But man's natural aggressive instinct, the hostility of each against all and of all against each, opposes this programme of civilization. . . . This struggle is what all life essentially consists of, and the evolution of civilization may therefore be simply described as the struggle for life of the human species.[1]

Freud felt that civilization represents an ever-increasing bonding between individuals working toward "one great unity of mankind." Civilization is opposed, however, by "man's aggressive instinct, the hostility of each against all and of all against each."

A point of view similar to Freud's is expressed in the writing of anthropologist Ruth Benedict:

> From all comparative material, the conclusion that emerges is that societies where non-aggression is conspicuous have social orders in which the individual by the same act and at the same time serves his own advantage and that of the group. . . . Non-aggression occurs (in these societies) not because people are unselfish and put social obligations above personal desires, but when social arrangements make these two identical. . . .
> I shall speak of cultures with low synergy where the social structure provides for acts which are mutually opposed and counteractive, and cultures with high synergy where it provides for acts which are mutually reinforcing.[2]

Benedict's concept of the synergistic society, where the social structure permits and encourages individual behaviors that are socially beneficial, is consistent with Freud's notion of civilization, where Eros, the unifying life-force, prevails.

Writing in a different and more difficult idiom in the field of philosophy, Martin Buber expresses a similar view in his concepts of the essential relationships of people, I-it and I-Thou.

> The one primary word is the combination "I-Thou." The other primary word is the combination "I-it." . . . The life of human beings is not passed in the sphere of transitive verbs alone. . . . I perceive something . . . I will something. I feel

something. I think something. The life of the human being does not consist of all this and the like alone. This and the like together establish the realm of "it." But the realm of "Thou" has a different basis. . . . For where there is a thing, there is another thing. Every "it" is bounded by others; "it" exists only through being bounded by others. But when "Thou" is spoken, there is no thing. "Thou" has no bounds.[3]

There is at work in the writings of all these theorists a sense of underlying conflict between opposing forces, one tending toward separateness and dissolution, the other toward integration. It is clear that at a given time there can be a tendency toward synergy or entropy, toward Eros or Thanatos, toward I-it or I-Thou. The optimist might contend that synergy or Eros or I-Thou is a reasonable goal for society; the pessimist may focus instead on the gathering power of the darker forces. Part of the commitment to social welfare arises in the optimistic belief that it can help society progress toward civilization or synergy or I-Thou, and simultaneously, that it can help decrease entropy, isolation, and deprivation. The question "How valuable is social welfare?" can be considered in these terms. Social welfare cannot, of course, complete these processes independently, but it should liberate them, encouraging the growth of positive energies and limiting the power of those that separate and destroy.

An important justification for social welfare, then, is that openness, synergy, and civilization are more likely to be achieved or approached in a society where individual and group needs are being met or where the opportunity exists for them to be met. Significant deprivation, whether physical or mental, can increase individuals' sense of isolation and alienation, thus leading to behaviors and attitudes that work against the integrative civilizing energies we have described as desirable.

The Hierarchy of Human Needs

Since the fulfillment of needs constitutes one important factor in social well-being, let us examine needs in their relationship to social welfare. Abraham Maslow has conceptualized a now-famous hierarchy of needs, beginning at the most basic level and rising to the state of psychological "self-actualization."

The first of Maslow's levels involves the fundamental biological requirements for survival: food, clothing, and shelter. These needs must be met, at least at a minimal level, before any higher needs can be fulfilled. Next come the "safety needs." This level involves the same biological essentials as level one but focuses on maintaining them once they are achieved rather than on acquiring them initially. Hence, satisfaction at this level implies a sense of security about the continued fulfillment of first-level needs.

What Maslow terms the higher-level needs begin with the third level, which he classifies as "love and belongingness." The fourth level is the "esteem need," including the desire for a firmly based and high evaluation of one's self, that is, a feeling of strength, mastery, and confidence that can lead to freedom and independence. The fifth and highest level is "self-actualization," which is achieved when someone is doing what he is capable of doing. "A musician must make music, an artist must paint, a poet must write if they are to be at peace with themselves. What a man can be he must be. This need we call self-actualization."

Maslow's thesis is that a preoccupation with lower-level needs that are unfulfilled stalls one's progression to the consideration of higher-level needs. If a man is starving, he will not be able to focus his energies on interpersonal relationships; if he is feeling rejected and unloved, he will not be able to proceed with the work of self-actualization.

Maslow's principal groupings, higher- and lower-level needs, basically reflect a division between the biological requirements for survival and the social/psychological rewards of relationships and achievement. Our contention, drawing on the insights of Freud, Benedict, Buber, and Maslow, is that the extent to which these higher- and lower-order needs can be met influences the extent to which synergy and civilization can occur. If food, clothing, shelter, and security are assured, the possibility of seeking esteem, confidence, self-worth, self-expression, and psychological well-being is enhanced; if these too are increased among larger numbers of people, Thanatos, the instinct toward dissolution and alienation, is decreased. Tendencies toward antisocial behavior are more likely to diminish if more members of the society are physically comfortable and psychologically at peace with themselves.

Human Needs and Social Welfare

Social welfare is designed to promote the fulfillment of human needs. That is the intent of its services. Some—the "hard services"—address the lower-order needs as defined by Maslow and provide the benefits that assure physical survival. Examples are Social Security, public assistance, unemployment insurance, job creation, food stamps, public housing, rent subsidies, Medicare, and Medicaid. Higher-order needs, related to social and psychological well-being, are met primarily through "soft services." Counseling and therapy, for example, address clients' attitudes, emotions, and relationships rather than their need for food, clothing, and shelter. Services for drug abuse, alcoholism, mental health, rehabilitation, and family therapy all strive to give the client increased confidence, self-esteem, understanding, and self-knowledge. The resource expended in the soft services is the human resource, an exchange between human beings. From a professional perspective, such an exchange involves the application of technique; but compassion, sensitivity, understanding, genuineness, and warmth may also be central to its efficacy. Soft services endeavor to diminish boundaries and decrease social distance, contributing to a sense of community and civilization.

Thus, through both hard services and soft, the social welfare institution seeks to inject into society a positive energy and to decrease the dehumanization and isolation that can cause or aggravate social problems. At least two other social institutions strive to achieve the same ends: the family and religion. But social welfare has been held in considerably lower esteem than either of these, especially in the recent past. It is, of course, far different in form. It is a public institution, created through public dollars; it has an almost artificial quality as compared to the family or to religion. It tends toward social intervention, which as we discussed in Chapter Two, runs counter to America's traditional values of self-reliance and individualism. Another point against it, from the perspective of public opinion, is the pervasive sense that has developed in recent years that social welfare is inefficient and ineffective. This, too, violates traditional values, such as efficiency and productivity. The institution cannot survive, no matter how well intended it is, if it appears to be out of synchrony with its society. In such a situation, the fundamental ideals and purposes of social welfare, which invite acceptance and support, are obscured by the perceived functioning of the institution in daily experience.

Social welfare must necessarily go against traditional values when it advocates social intervention; it cannot afford to sustain the additional burden of being seen as ineffective and unproductive. Unfortunately, this has become a widespread perception, and with it has surfaced the most fundamental question of policy: Do we dismantle, reduce, or even abandon the basic concept of a social welfare institution, or do we reaffirm our belief in the potential benefit to society of such a public endeavor? The latter course, we believe, is the right one to take. However, certain changes in philosophy, approach, structure, and design are necessary in order that this may be achieved.

NEW WAYS OF THINKING ABOUT SOCIAL WELFARE

Throughout this book we have argued that there is an imbalance in the social welfare institution that is causing it to tilt too far in directions that threaten to tear it apart. In the remainder of this chapter and through the next, we will discuss the directions in which we believe the social welfare institution must move in order to avoid this danger. If the social welfare institution is fundamentally beneficial to society, as we have argued, and if it is currently lacking both cohesion and general support, how should it be changed? We believe that changes need to occur on two levels: (1) attitudes and ideas and (2) structure and policy. In this chapter we shall discuss the first level; in Chapter Nine we will make more specific recommendations at the level of structure and policy.

Let us begin, then, with some of the conceptual changes we believe must take place before reforms at the more practical level can be expected or effectively implemented. We will present a brief summary of our recommendations in the area of social welfare concepts and then discuss them one by one:

1. Social welfare must come to be seen as a permanent and stable part of American life.
2. Social welfare must be conceptualized as a holistic structure that serves all members of the society, not a charity program for the poor or an assortment of exclusive benefits for narrowly defined groups.
3. The temporizing values of service, compassion, and opportunity must be reasserted as important elements of the American value system.
4. Human service technology must make room for reconstructive as well as rehabilitative approaches to social problems; systems as well as individual clients must become the objects of social intervention.
5. While aspects of social welfare benefit from decentralization and local autonomy, it is important that the overall pattern of the social welfare institution move toward greater coordination and centralization.

The Permanence and Stability of the
Social Welfare Institution

As we have observed throughout this book, America's approach to the provision of social welfare has generally been both tentative and inconsistent. We have tried to show that this approach is expressed in values—how Americans think about the social welfare institution; in technology—how they choose to intervene in social problems; and in structure—how the social welfare institution is organized. Recent tilts toward more traditional values, more rehabilitative technologies, and more decentralized structures have combined to create a social welfare institution characterized by the following tendencies:

1. Treatment approaches that emphasize client deficiencies
2. Perception of social interventions as time limited and emergency based
3. Incremental approach to planning
4. Heavy emphasis on fiscal accountability.

We would contend that the first change needed to improve the effectiveness of the social welfare institution is at the level of social philosophy, the nation's basic thinking about social problems and programs. The tentativeness of America's commitment to the social welfare institution simply does not reflect the reality of the social problems the institution is designed to address. They are not temporary. The issues addressed by the hard services (unemployment, lack of income, lack of housing, lack of clothing, lack of medical care) and those addressed by the soft services (alcoholism, drug abuse, violence, child abuse, mental illness, developmental disabilities) are not fleeting phenomena that will soon disappear in accordance with some natural course. They have been with us, and they continue to be with us. The social welfare institution, no matter how large and no matter what its level of public and financial support, can only be effective if it reflects a stable and continuing recognition of social need.

It is, of course, far easier to assert what needs to be done than to point to ways in which it can be done. We are referring here solely to the domain of thoughts and attitudes. The process by which such attitudes are translated into policies that can be tested, debated, and embodied in programs will be explored in the next chapter. At this point our principal contention is that changes in attitude toward social welfare are the essential first step that must precede more concrete reforms. Only when the social welfare institution achieves recognition as a continuing and integral element in the fabric of American society can other necessary changes follow.

A Holistic and Universal Concept of Social Welfare

Besides recognizing the permanence of the social welfare institution and the problems that it confronts, there is a need for a holistic concept of social welfare, a movement in our thinking toward a more inclusive and universalistic notion of the institution and the people it is designed to serve. Obviously, we are not referring to the abandonment of specialization; our concern is rather over the degree to which specialization now dominates the field of social welfare. We need to move closer to the idea that the social welfare institution, a public institution created by and through public deliberation and funded through public dollars, is responsible for serving the whole society, albeit in different ways and at different times. Income maintenance programs, therefore, need to be viewed as part of the same system, the same set of social policies, as, for example, programs that provide marital counseling or long-term psychiatric care. The distinctions often set up by the institution itself and by the way in which it is organized—the separating of people and their problems into isolated categories—need to be diminished, if the objectives of social welfare are to be more fully realized.

In recent years, as we noted in Chapters Five and Six, there has been a reversal of the previous movement toward more unitary or centralized approaches to social welfare, both in program concept and organizational design. The result has been balkanization, a loss of the sense of the whole, a fragmentation of effort and a corresponding loss of public support. Influenced perhaps too strongly by contemporary norms of participation and noninterventionism, the social welfare institution has weakened its claim to other important values; it has become less efficient, less productive, and—most important—seemingly less able to facilitate the well-being of society as a whole. This has contributed to its political vulnerability and eroding support. Some of those who generally favor social welfare have themselves adopted a more decentralized and particularistic approach in recent years; these trends have tended to reinforce the views of those who have always opposed unitary and centralized systems of social welfare. Hence, the historic movement toward an institution that is more and more inclusive, involving increasingly holistic and centralized views of social welfare, has had no recent organized advocacy.

In essence, a holistic approach toward the social welfare institution would represent a transformation, a reversal in thinking that could lead to a reenergizing. Such an approach is based on the reemergence of what in Chapter Two we termed the consensual value of social well-being. This is the agreed-upon value that each person should have adequate food, clothing, and shelter, plus some sense of self-worth and nurturance. Americans in this century have for the most part committed themselves to this idea. Few oppose this fundamental consensual value, except, perhaps, libertarians of the right who believe in the strict social Darwinist notion that *no* intervention of an organized nature should take place and radicals of the extreme left who would hold that any social intervention, by temporarily improving social conditions, delays the needed revolution, which is the only road to meaningful change.

Aside from these purists at either end of the spectrum, however, most Americans would subscribe to the idea that some social intervention is necessary to ensure social well-being. The difference, as we argued in Chapter Two, is one of degree, with the traditional values tending to favor as little intervention as possible, while the temporizing position argues that more intervention is necessary to alleviate social problems.

Fundamentally, the New Deal programs of the 1930s reflected a more universal tone than those of more recent times. The Social Security Act met the needs of millions; unemployment insurance and old-age benefits provided a safety net under the insecurity that much of the population feared. That widespread coverage is the basis of support for a universalistic social program, because it creates and maintains a broad-based constituency, almost by definition. Its social effect is cohesive, stressing common problems and potential insecurities, and not divisive, singling out special groups and setting the stage for rivalry and competition.

A few of the Great Society programs—Medicare, Medicaid, and civil rights legislation—have survived for similar reasons. In some ways they are more oriented to specific groups than the New Deal programs; for instance, they set up two distinct systems of medical care reimbursement, with Medicaid being lower status than Medicare, since Medicaid serves only the poor. Nevertheless, these programs have survived because they addressed deeply felt needs of large numbers of people. Many more specifically targeted Great Society programs have virtually disappeared. The fact that programs started fifty years ago have survived and become a strong part of the social welfare institution, while the programs of the Great Society have for the most part fared less well, underscores the case for a more universalistic approach. It is clear that even from the most basic political view, programs that define their constituencies by strict demographics, such as age or race, or by individual problems, such as legal aid, are by definition more exclusive and less able to build a strong constituency, because each stands alone.

The need to develop a more holistic view of social welfare, to move toward universalism in program concept, seems necessary, then, because it can help foster the view of social welfare as a single system for enhancing the well-being of the whole society; in addition, more broad-based political and social support can be engendered by such an approach. Finally, this approach promises a more pragmatic and effective way of attacking social problems, reducing the inefficiency of recent years.

As the concept of the social welfare institution as an integral part of American life takes hold and is reinforced by an emphasis on approaches and programs that serve a wide range of Americans, certain more specific attitudinal changes can be expected as well. These altered perspectives on values, technology, and structure are essential if the social welfare policy pendulum is to swing back to a viewpoint more favorable to its development.

Reassessing of Temporizing Values

Attacks on the social welfare institution in recent years have focused on its means, not its ends. Criticism has centered on the kinds of programs offered, who they benefit, and how they have run. There has been little disagreement over the humanitarian intent of the institution. In fact, the institution's goals have rarely been attacked by opponents of social welfare; but neither have they been persuasively articulated by its proponents and advocates. In effect, social welfare's overall purposes have been only peripherally a part of public debate; in general, the fundamental case for social welfare has not been made. The values of sensitivity, compassion, and opportunity have rarely been given the constructive and compelling forum they merit; for the most part, traditional values have received more vigorous expression, more frequent exposition. The case has been made that traditional values represent a viable path to the consensual value of social well-being. This, we would argue, has affected the social policy pendulum. The temporizing values, in order to redress the imbalance, also need to be linked to the consensual value of social well-being and firmly reasserted.

It is the reassertion of temporizing values that legitimizes the social welfare institution and provides it with its energy. But the case needs to be made that these values do not mean the repudiation of traditional values. As we have noted, the link needs to be made with efficiency, with self-reliance, with freedom. The pursuit of compassion or sensitivity is not a process antithetical to these values. Just as opponents of social welfare argue that the temporizing goals can be achieved in the context of traditional means, so the argument needs to be made that values such as compassion and pragmatism can also coexist. This, of course, is far easier to assert than to achieve. But such a balance is a necessity if social welfare is to gain support in the context of the overall attitudes and values of society. Only by striking a new and more constructive balance between the practicality of traditional values and the humanity of temporizing values can the reform of the social welfare institution proceed.

Toward a More Reconstructive Policy Premise

Americans' tentative and inconsistent approach to social welfare in recent years has led to the almost total abandonment of what we have termed the reconstructive policy premise in human service technology. Clients, not systems or structures, have become the principal focus of social intervention. The effort to resolve social problems has tended increasingly to proceed on a narrowly defined, case-by-case basis. This lack of broader vision has further depleted the energy of the social welfare institution and has fed the problems of fragmentation and waning support that we have described. The tilt toward rehabilitative technologies has set certain other mechanisms in motion as well, shaping program objectives and organizational design along similar lines.

Again, a holistic view that sees beyond the immediate case to the need for changes in the social structure has been nearly absent. Documents with reconstructive points of view, such as England's Beveridge Report or even the task force reports of the late sixties, have virtually disappeared. There has been no new thrust in social welfare such as the Medicare/Medicaid program or the establishment of Community Mental Health Centers in two decades. Even calls for welfare reform, such as Nixon's and Carter's, have fallen silent. In 1984, for the first time in forty years, the Democratic platform failed to include a plank calling for some system of national health insurance. Without this kind of initiative and vision, the institution as a whole suffers.

As we have argued, the present approach to technology, emphasizing highly specialized technical skills, may have carried us closer to rehabilitative, case-specific concepts of service. More refined and professionalized notions of the treatment of individual problems have tended to favor the casework model and may have played some part in dissipating staff's openness to reconstructive approaches. Again, this is a matter of tilt, of balance; neither approach should be adopted exclusively in preference to the other. But the present imbalance in the direction of rehabilitative technologies has to some extent weakened the institution.

Obviously, the pursuit of social well-being by the social welfare institution needs to reflect both rehabilitative and reconstructive policy premises, just as it must reflect both temporizing and traditional values. In the final analysis, social welfare policies and programs need to serve individuals, to meet their needs, and to improve the quality of their lives socially, psychologically, and culturally. Such service must always be the goal. The focus of intervention to achieve that goal, however, may vary. Sometimes the client may need assistance; in other cases the systems that affect the client are the appropriate locus of intervention. As was the case with values, what needs to be redressed to move the pendulum of policy is the balance between the two premises. Neither the rehabilitative nor the reconstructive approach should prevail exclusively; both should be drawn upon to enrich the repertory of human service technology available to address social problems.

More Centralized Authority

As we have noted, the recent disposition toward decentralization and local autonomy may have exacted too high a price in terms of the social welfare institution's effectiveness. An important question needs to be addressed: Can a complex institution such as social welfare function effectively with a highly decentralized structure? We have argued that such a structure has caused problems both in coordinating program policy and in attracting public support. Again, we are not arguing for a complete move toward centralization; such a move would dissipate the positive effects that can accompany local autonomy and initiative. As with values and structure, the challenge is to redress an imbalance. Too much decentralization, we believe, has tended to reinforce the fragmented and temporary quality of the institution as it stands today; a nationally consistent, more centralized system would be less vulnerable to such problems.

Here, too, the overview has been lost; holistic approaches have been submerged in the multiple interests of the organizations and organizational levels that have come into play. It is unlikely that the Department of Defense, for instance, would expect to achieve its goals with such a structure. The idea of thousands of local or county Defense Departments, responsible through several, often conflicting avenues of accountability to a variety of state and federal departments, is difficult to conceive. Nor would a large corporation allow its local units total autonomy in priority setting, product design, and marketing. Yet the public investment in social welfare has been moving increasingly in such a direction.

As we have argued, the tradition of social welfare until the mid-1960s represented movement in the general direction of increasing national commitment to and organization of social welfare. This was also true in the Progressive Era and in the New Deal. Beginning in the 1960s the structural emphasis was on federal initiative combined with increasing responsibility for implementation at the local level. This change was instituted to avoid what were seen as the bureaucratic rigidities of the intervening layers of government. In a sense, we are urging an approach that moves closer to the concepts of the earlier eras, tipping the balance more in the direction of a national organizational design. In

Chapter Nine we will outline some specific proposals that we believe would help achieve that tilt without losing the benefits of local initiative where they are most productive.

A New Balance

What we have proposed in this chapter is a reassertion of a tradition that spans nearly a century. The approach calls, not for a radical departure, but for the striking of a new balance. We have argued for a renewed emphasis on certain concepts fundamental to social welfare: recognition of the permanence of our social problems, a move toward a more holistic concept of social welfare, the reaffirmation of the consensual value of social well-being as the basic philosophical tenet of social welfare, a reassertion of temporizing values, a move toward reconstructive perspectives, and a return to more centralized structures of organization and delivery. These recommendations are based on the idea that the social welfare institution can be reformed, can, in fact, reassert its traditional legitimacy, and can function in harmony with the values of effectiveness and pragmatism, while maintaining a fundamental commitment to temporizing values of humanity and mutual support. Most importantly, we believe that the social welfare institution can help alleviate social problems and help society move closer to the levels of synergy and civilization described by Freud, Benedict, Maslow, and Buber.

What we are suggesting, the reformation of an institution, is a difficult endeavor. But the current functioning of the institution is often at odds with its humanitarian intent. As we have argued, the opponents of the institution have often criticized the *form* of American social welfare, but rarely its *intent*. Yet the form, the instrument that carries out the intent, must be consistent with the values and attitudes of the society in which it functions. If the institution is out of congruence or is perceived to be, then it cannot survive. What we have suggested here, the redressing of imbalances within the institution, is based on the analysis we have presented throughout the book. Our approach in this chapter has dealt with ideas and attitudes. In the book's final chapter, we will present some policy suggestions that follow from this approach.

SUMMARY

We began this chapter with an exploration of the benefits that social welfare can offer society. Reviewing the work of Freud, Benedict, Buber, and Maslow, we argued that social welfare increases the level of civilization and synergy in society, fosters the more outreaching "I-Thou" relationship, and addresses the human needs that can inhibit social well-being. Survival needs—such as food, clothing, shelter, and security—are generally met through social welfare's "hard services," including cash and in-kind benefits. The higher needs, as defined by Maslow, include satisfying social relationships and feelings of psychological self-worth and are addressed through the "soft services," such as counseling and therapy.

In order for the social welfare institution to improve its effectiveness and its level of public support, we have contended that certain changes are necessary in the way Americans think about social problems and social welfare. The institution must be seen as a permanent and stable element in American life, not simply a periodic source of emergency help. A more universal view of the institution must also be developed, so that its services are seen as part of a single holistic system, undivided by class, demographic, or economic categorizations. Temporizing values must be reasserted, not to the exclusion of traditional values, but so that they hold an equally important place in Americans' thinking. Rehabilitative technologies must no longer hold center stage in human service technology; room must be made for reconstructive approaches to social welfare as well. Finally, a more centralized organizational design for social welfare must be considered, one that will give ample room for local initiative and energy yet regain some of the advantages of nationally consistent and coordinated approaches to social welfare.

Vehicles for Change

In the preceding chapter we made the argument for a reexamination of current thinking about the social welfare institution. One possible next step would be to propose a series of programs based on reconstructive premises or holistic concepts, which might serve to exemplify what we have recommended. Such programs are very much needed and have been proposed often in the past. We believe, however, that in order for them to contribute to the overall effectiveness of the social welfare institution, they must be seen as part of a broader system and be instituted in the context of more fundamental changes at the structural level.

In this chapter, therefore, we will turn our attention not to the individual programs that are surely required, but to the functioning of the institution itself. We will suggest changes and vehicles for change that reflect and advance our analysis. These are by no means intended to offer a blueprint for change; such a claim would be both presumptuous and premature. The structural approaches that we propose would instead represent the beginning of a process through which the whole system of social welfare could be gradually strengthened. They reflect in terms of policy and organization the kind of general directions our analysis has suggested.

In Chapter One we discussed two processes that appear to play a major part in the movement of the social policy pendulum. One is the outside process, in which those outside the social welfare institution—recipient groups, those who work on their behalf, advocacy organizations, scholars, journalists, and a host of others—help bring about social change through a combination of advocacy, public education, and political activism. Inside the social welfare institution, a complementary process is necessary, in which insiders devote their political, professional, and administrative resources to furthering the process of change and reform.

In this chapter we will suggest changes in both arenas that we believe will heighten their effectiveness and thus the ability of the social welfare institution to benefit society.

THE INSIDE PROCESS

What we will propose in the next several pages are vehicles and structures that we believe will help to alleviate the problems and dysfunctions in the social welfare institution that we have identified throughout our analysis. We do not, of course, maintain that these changes can be easily attained. But we do contend that such changes and others like them need to be part of the next swing of the pendulum.

As we have observed, during the Progressive Era and the 1930s, the pendulum swung into what could be considered almost a structural vacuum. Little existed in the way of public program and organization. What was created was new. This provided an opportunity for the planners and early implementers of programs to work relatively unencumbered by previous structures. As we have noted, the programs of the 1960s constituted a departure because they had to contend with programs, bureaucracies, turfs, and interests that were already in place, making the process more politicized and less open to rational conception and planning. The current structure is even more developed than it was in the early 1960s. Indeed, the complexity of existing interrelationships is so great that any new swing of the pendulum commences with far fewer degrees of freedom than has been the case in the past. Therefore, before new programs can be implemented to address the social problems of our society, structural reforms are necessary to deal with the programs and policies already in place. Any new initiative that does not take this requirement into account runs the risk of aggravating the unwieldiness of present structures and thus diminishing the very aspects of the social welfare institution that it had intended to improve: its effectiveness and its level of public support.

Hard and Soft Services: A Structural Proposal

As noted in the previous chapter, social welfare seeks to address two sets of needs. The lower-order needs (as defined by Maslow)—food, shelter, and clothing—are met by the provision of hard services in the form of cash transfers and in-kind benefits, such as food stamps, reimbursement for health care, and public housing. The soft services address Maslow's higher-order needs by seeking to improve individual's social functioning and to help them achieve a degree of psychological satisfaction and well-being. These are the benefits that the social welfare institution can help society achieve; taken together, they constitute the condition of social well-being, which, as we discussed in Chapter One, is a consensual value of most societies.

Hard and soft services involve different kinds of exchanges. The resources distributed through the hard services are tangible, finite, quantified, and accountable. They include food, money, and living space. They tend to be redistributive in nature and less specialized to particular problems or clients than soft services. Providing money to someone in California through Social Security, for example, is the same basic exchange as making a public assistance payment in Mississippi. The actual nature of the service is identical, although the circumstances surrounding the two exchanges, the eligibility requirements, and the social meaning they hold for staff and recipient may vary significantly.

The exchange in soft services is very different. Involving as it does human perceptions, attitudes, and emotions, it is far less quantifiable, accountable, or even tangible than the hard services. Its purpose is to humanize relationships, increase openness between people, and, in a very real sense, help heighten the degree of civilization described in Chapter Eight.

As we discussed in Chapter Three, the resource involved in soft services combines professional expertise with a more indefinable exchange of caring and emotion. It is very difficult to discern precisely where one ends and the other begins. At the turn of the century the exchange was thought to be a process of moral education, where caseworkers or friendly visitors gave of their own moral character to the poor. Now the exchange is considered more in terms of professional expertise based on scientific principles. But whatever the interaction, the goal of soft services remains in the social/psychological domain, and the outcome, if successful, contributes to the same aspects of the client's life.

The differing nature of these two services, hard and soft, suggests that they may require different forms of organization. The soft service is more individualized, needing a comparatively unstructured organizational environment, a freedom to explore, so that the exchange may find its proper level. The hard service is more standardized; the provision of tangible resources like food, income, or housing can benefit from a more formal structure. In essence, it does not matter who it is that writes the check for the recipient as long as it is in the right amount. The soft services, to be effective, require the fostering of a delicate and fragile human relationship.

Because of these differences, we propose that the structural form of the social welfare institution should follow its function. It should reflect in organizational design the nature of the particular kind of service provided. A structure based on the nature of service is far different from one designed simply to mediate different levels of government, or fulfill the bureaucratic interests of different organizational constituencies, or fit jagged pieces of service together, or satisfy the attempts of various groups to compete for funds. What we have lost in the way the institution has evolved structurally in the past few years is a consideration of the kind of service that the structure is designed to deliver. It has been difficult to approach freshly this central question: What kind of structure can best deliver each particular kind of service?

What we are proposing reflects the overall directions that we presented in Chapter Eight. A more holistic approach, we believe, would serve to decrease fragmentation and would provide more effective service; in addition, it would help to integrate social groups rather than divide them. In essence, we propose a more centralized structure for the provision of all hard services and a more community-based (though integrated) structure for the provision of soft services.

The Hard Services

The current organization of the hard services can be viewed as follows:

Social Insurance	Public Charity
Federal Programs	
Old Age Survivorship	Veterans Benefits
Permanent Disability (OASDI)	Institutional Care in
Medicare	Federal Districts
SSI	
Federal Employees Benefits	
Railroad Employees Benefits	
Federal-State Programs	
Unemployment Insurance	AFDC
	Medicaid
	Food Stamps
	Housing
State-Local Programs	
Workmen's Compensation	Institutional Care
Temporary Disability	Supplementary Welfare
State and Local Employees	Benefits
Benefits	

We are proposing that the model of Social Security be utilized for all income transfer programs, both cash and in-kind, to the extent that this is possible. This change would, of course, be achieved in different degrees at different times, but it represents a policy direction toward which the social welfare institution should move. Programs would follow the lines of a comprehensive social insurance system and would avoid the invidious distinctions currently at work that have set up competing systems for the poor and the rest of society, as in Social Security versus public assistance and Medicare versus Medicaid. In its most comprehensive form, this concept, by no means new, would integrate all the hard services—such as Social Security, unemployment insurance, unemployment compensation, aid to the blind and disabled, Medicare, Medicaid, food stamps, rent supplements, and energy assistance—and federalize their implementation. Thus the local offices would be federal offices implementing nationally consistent policies, as is the case in Social Security, and not state, city, or regional offices with different policies according to their jurisdictions.

This plan would, in a sense, reassert the tradition of social welfare suggested in the Progressive Era and established through the New Deal; the federal government would be the implementer of services that address national concerns. Such an approach grows from the principle that the income needs of people are not individualized as to locality, state, or region, but are part of a national condition and should be viewed from a national perspective.

Obviously, such an approach is debatable; it reverses a trend toward the decentralization of services that has been growing over the past few years. We would argue that such a reversal would carry many advantages. First, it would simplify the structure considerably. Arguments for the guaranteed income, the negative income tax, the Family Assistance Plan proposed by Nixon, and the Program for Better Jobs and Income proposed by Carter have often made this point. Second, it would make the allocation of services more equitable. The current differences in grants, as discussed in Chapter Six, are enormous, and difficult to explain rationally; a national program would better meet the goal of equity. Finally, from the perspective of the analysis presented throughout this book, this social insurance approach is more holistic and integrative with regard to both program and recipient, tending to diminish the distinctions between groups and eliminate the overlapping and inconsistent categories of income maintenance. Recipients would receive varying amounts of assistance depending on their levels of need, but they would not be grouped into different classes of service for these reasons.

The support of such a direction for the hard services stands in contradiction to trends in popular belief during the past several decades. We would argue, however, that the fragmentation, duplication, and inefficiency that have existed are a serious threat to the strength of the social welfare institution. Obviously, the complete integration and federalization of the hard services is not a practical immediate objective for the social welfare institution. Formally advocating such an idea, generating public support for it, and ultimately implementing it would, of course, be an enormous task. What we are recommending is that this again become the *direction* for policy.

It does seem apparent that the problems of income maintenance, housing, food, and health care are permanent ones. Thus a structure that recognizes this permanence and offers a single efficient national system for addressing such needs would reduce the divisions between social groups, decrease inefficient and invidious categorization, and win more consistent support from the larger community. Such a structure would reflect a unitary concern for social well-being, rather than a combination of social insurance for some groups and more low-status charity for others. It would serve to strengthen the social welfare institution as a respected element of American society, allowing it to serve a more integrative function rather than labeling individuals differently depending on whether they receive public assistance or Medicaid, Social Security or SSI.

Clearly, making all income transfers unitary and federal, based on the general system of social insurance, would require a long process of advocacy and change; we are not necessarily arguing for wholesale acceptance of this approach. There would certainly be significant administrative problems, not the least of which would be the reordering of bureaucratic structures. Instead, we contend that this needs to be the *direction* of the reform of the hard services and of future reorganizations of the social welfare institution. To the extent that reform begins to move in this direction, we believe that the institution's ability to benefit society will be strengthened.

Reforming the Soft Services

As we have noted, the nature of the exchange of soft services requires a different organizational structure from that appropriate for hard services. A centralized federal structure for providing mental health, drug abuse, child abuse, or alcoholism treatment would not, we believe, increase their effectiveness. Such centralization would make little sense, given the nature of the services themselves, the need for individualizing treatment, and the kinds of technologies involved. In addition, the soft services require a high degree of integration between service and community, which is less likely to be needed in the case of hard services. The need to involve community systems such as the family, the work place, school, private agencies, self-help groups, and local governmental structures requires that the soft services be based at the local community level. The social problems addressed by the soft services are often so entwined with the life of the local community that planning and delivery need to take place at that level. We would argue, then, for a more decentralized structure for the soft services, but an approach that emphasizes local coherence and cohesiveness.

In the past few decades, soft services have multiplied at the local level, although often on a very fragmented basis. As we have noted throughout the book, services for individual groups—such as alcoholics, drug abusers, the developmentally disabled, the mentally ill—are far more fully developed and available at the community level now than they were in earlier years. This is the legacy of the 1960s swing of the pendulum. Although, as we have argued, the programs of that period were frequently unsuccessful in solving the problems they addressed, they did help establish a strong tradition of community participation and involvement that has continued into the 1980s. If the social welfare institution as a whole is to be strengthened in the way we feel is needed, these processes and developments at the local level need to be built upon.

We would contend that one necessity in the soft services is to identify integrative technologies, to build upon commonalities in service delivery. Are there elements in the exchange between a client and a therapist in a drug abuse program that are similar to those of a program for runaway youth? Are any similar kinds of services offered in group homes for the mentally ill and the developmentally disabled? In the hard services, as we have noted, the exchange is simply the disbursement of cash or in-kind benefits. But perhaps the exchange in these soft-services programs also has some common elements. We believe that organizational and delivery structures should begin to reflect the holistic nature of the service and place less emphasis on problem-specific responses to highly differentiated constituencies. It is a matter of balance.

A strong, permanent social welfare institution that gains and keeps public support cannot function effectively with rigidly separate programs for the aging, youth, the developmentally disabled, the mentally ill, drug abusers, women, Indians, the homeless, runaways, and abused children, particularly if these programs are further divided depending on whether they are offered in clinics, hospitals, supervised residences, or outreach sites. Maintaining such a variety of separate services inevitably heightens the danger of duplication, of delivering similar services through complex and unwieldy parallel structures that obstruct rather than facilitate client care.

Let us consider an example. A family in crisis in New York State must deal with the Department of Social Services for income maintenance, the Office of Mental Health for counseling, the Division of Alcohol Abuse for alcoholism services, the Council for Children and Families for advocacy, and then back to the Department of Social Services for child-abuse issues. A youth in trouble may need a range of services provided by the Division for Youth, the Department of Corrections, the court system, the school system, the Office of Mental Health, the Division of Substance Abuse, the Division of Alcohol Abuse, and the Department of Labor. Because agencies frequently have difficulty integrating their efforts, the recipient is pulled apart and may receive only a few of the services he or she needs, provided in a fragmented and perhaps duplicative manner that reduces still further their effectiveness. When integration does occur, it is likely to be based on informal contacts between staff rather than on systematic and formal relationships between agencies.

A human service center might offer one way of bringing together those service elements that could be logically integrated from the perspective of technology and organizational structure. Instead of having parallel streams of funding moving down a large number of different competing and often isolated routes, complementary human service structures could be instituted at regional and state levels to integrate planning and funding of related services. What is most important, however, is the community level, the point at which the actual service is delivered. Here a center that integrated service approaches could treat the client more holistically. It would also serve to bridge social groups. The elderly, youth, minorities, and others would be encouraged by this structure to see the human needs they shared, rather than those that set them apart. The problems of depression or family violence or unemployment might be viewed not as issues requiring specific services for one group alone, but more as problems that are shared by many in different demographic categories. Approaching service in this way might help also to solidify the alliances among groups outside the social welfare institution whose efforts we have described as "the outside process." This point will be explored further in a later section of this chapter.

Considering the possibility of human service centers raises the question of specialized technologies and differentiated clienteles. A comparison with the services of a general hospital might serve best to illustrate the human service center concept. A general hospital provides a wide range of medical services to a wide range of patients. Medical specialties are available to those who suffer from particular ailments, and they are present within one organization. While there are individual departments of cardiology, orthopedics, and so on, they function as elements of a single administrative unit, the hospital, and make few *clinical* distinctions between old and young, black and white, male and female. Thus, patient, medical problem, and medical technology are brought together in one organizational system. Obviously there are exceptions, such as nursing homes, hospices, and specialized hospitals for highly technical treatment of particular diseases, but for the most part the general hospital is the model.

To set up a different kind of community health system—with different hospitals for different demographic groups, different ages, different sexes, different races, and different diseases—would create the kind of disorganization that exists now in the human services. Administering the human services so as to emphasize the commonalities inherent in different technologies, social problems, and client groups would benefit the social welfare institution, and it might also add potency to the outside process by bringing disparate groups together.

Of course, we are not advocating the elimination of separate specialties any more than a general hospital would merge cardiology and orthopedics. Rather, a human service center would offer services to youth, to the aging, and to the mentally ill, combining those aspects that could be merged but allowing for specialization in those aspects that from a technical perspective should remain separate. We are suggesting that services move more in the direction of holistic and comprehensive treatment—not that specialized approaches be abandoned.

In order for the human service center concept to be effective, currently disparate technologies and services would need to be examined for commonalities and differences. Obviously, perfect organizational design is not attainable, but, to the extent possible, organization structures should reflect the true nature of technology and service exchange. If similar interactions are occurring in two or more service exchanges that are currently isolated and that serve several different client groups, a more integrative approach might be indicated, supported by the kind of organizational design that could facilitate the most effective delivery of the service. If an analysis of the service shows that different exchanges are occurring in different service settings, then specialized approaches may be important. But it is essential to assess each service in this way, identifying and maximizing common ground. Each service unit of a hospital, for example, does not require its own X-ray unit. A single radiology department can assist with the treatment of cancer or heart problems or broken bones. Do human services possess similar approaches that can help to integrate efforts clinically and organizationally?

It is far beyond the scope of this book to attempt to resolve or even systematically examine this question. The answer lies where policy analysis and program planning meet clinical treatment. From the perspective of this book, one common element is clear and perhaps could serve as the point of departure. All exchanges in the soft services are expected to include elements of sensitivity, compassion, empathy, genuineness, and social support. This is a fundamental aspect of the soft services. It can be contended that it is these exchanges, as much as the accompanying expertise, that alleviate individual social problems, that it is these exchanges which the individual client really seeks, and that professional technique is simply the means by which this transfer of positive energy is facilitated. The opposite could also be argued—that the application of professional technique is simply facilitated by the exchange of warmth, empathy, and so on, and that it is such techniques that alleviate social problems. That question is impossible for us to resolve here.

But the openness, the honesty, the genuineness, and compassion of the soft-service exchange do reflect a commonality that cuts across different services and may be a place to begin a search for a more integrative approach. The linked analysis of technique, human interaction, and social problems might begin to suggest which current technologies need to remain specialized and which can be integrated. Our point is that some degree of integration, of holistic overview, is needed and that organizational structures need to be altered so that they will reflect more accurately the actual nature of service and service exchange, rather than simply mirroring the traditions and customs of the organizational and bureaucratic status quo.

Our proposals for both the hard and soft services require an overview, an holistic perspective that views the institution as a single system. The current structure almost prohibits such a view by making it difficult for those in the inside process to see across client groups, technologies, and individual organizations and agencies and to begin asking the kinds of questions that lead to holistic solutions. But small-scale reform can make larger-scale reform possible. It is our belief that if the movement toward service integration begins—whether in relation to more centralization of hard services at the federal level or more integration of soft services at the local level—broader reform along similar lines will follow.

A Council of Social Advisers

The subject of social welfare as a whole—an analysis of its programs, the social problems it confronts, its objectives and goals, and its progress and priorities—needs greater and more sustained national attention. Social welfare needs to become a more significant part of American thought and policy debate; it needs a vehicle by which it can begin to gain a share of attention comparable to that given to other important aspects of contemporary life, such as defense, foreign policy, or the economy.

We propose the creation of a Council of Social Advisers (CSA), to serve as a counterpart of the President's Council of Economic Advisers (CEA). Such a council would serve as the focal point of the nation's concerns about social issues and social policy in much the same manner that the CEA does for the economy and economic policy. Like the CEA, the CSA would operate outside the current bureaucratic structure; it would have no turf to defend and no administrative or funding objectives to pursue. It would be composed of three members and supported by a staff of experts in the social sciences and the human services. Cooperating closely with a wide network of knowledgeable analysts in government, the academic community, and industry, the council would be responsible for gathering, analyzing, and interpreting information about the nation's social condition in order to assess our current success in meeting social goals and to establish priorities for national policy and program.

The CSA would thus become an important resource in helping to analyze the social impact of present and proposed programs. This would be of particular value when, as happens increasingly, program impact crosses departmental and/or government lines. Furthermore, under the current structure of social welfare, social problems often arise in different areas which can only be resolved by a unified approach that observes neither turf nor special interests. In such cases, the knowledge and counsel of a group of experts without institutional commitment to a single set of solutions could greatly facilitate the development of a fresh and integrated response.

As focus for its efforts, the Council would be responsible for working with the President to prepare an annual President's Social Report to Congress, the social counterpart to the President's Economic Report. In this report the President would detail the overall progress and effectiveness of federal efforts to implement social policies; review state, local, and private efforts toward the same ends; and present recommendations for the coming year.

To prepare the President's Economic Report, the Council of Economic Advisers has had to develop a system of economic criteria to measure the present and prospective conditions of the economy. It has increased the expertise and the rigor of the economics discipline in order to reduce the margin of error in economic measures, and it has developed tools of economic analysis, calling upon the entire community of economists for contributions. It has had to proceed with caution so as to command the respect and acceptance of decision makers, and its recommendations and findings have had to be action oriented. The same process is now appropriate and necessary in the social endeavors of the federal government.

The annual social report prepared by the CSA might be broken down on the basis of different kinds of social problems, what is being done to combat them, and the relative effectiveness of such efforts. This could help bring attention to the issues and add influence to the social welfare institution; it would contribute in an organized way to the recognition of social problems and help publicize possible solutions for addressing them. The council could also assess the impact of other governmental actions, such as tax policy or immigration legislation, on social problems and the human services.

While preparation of the social report would be an annual responsibility, the CSA would also play an ongoing role in the analysis and discussion of social issues. It would help set priorities for the social welfare institution, explore the interrelationships of problems and service approaches, serve as a focal point for the communication of social concerns to the general public, provide a clearinghouse for statistics and studies on a variety of social questions, and offer informed and rational comment on social issues as they arose.

The council could also serve in a mediating role between different parts of the social welfare institution, promoting linkage and exchange from a service perspective rather than having these exchanges dominated by fiscal and administrative considerations. For example, if an innovative program is being tried in one state, information about it could be communicated across administrative and geographic boundaries to others for whom it might be helpful. Currently, there is no single point in the social welfare institution where the encouragement of such communications takes place in an organized, structured way.

In the first chapter we noted that the tradition of expansion and reform in social welfare, including both the inside and outside processes, has fluctuated over time, with different eras being characterized by different approaches to social welfare, different levels of commitment, and different proposals. A structural development such as the creation of a Council of Social Advisers might help stabilize these cycles. Outside groups pressing for social change could benefit from having a place where statistics and proposals from other times and other areas were available. Those working in the universities, where innovative research and proposals often develop but fail to catch the attention of policy makers, would have better access to a public forum for their work. Above all, this proposal—like others we have offered—would facilitate an overview, helping to unify presently scattered energies in order to strengthen the social welfare institution and the potential benefits it can bring to society.

THE OUTSIDE PROCESS

Throughout this book we have discussed the balkanization of the social welfare institution. We have also described a similar pattern among the groups outside the social welfare institution that press for change and for a more equitable distribution of society's resources. During the past fifteen to twenty years, we have noted, the outside process has appeared to suffer from a lack of cohesion and coherence. That is, individual groups such as women or the elderly or blacks or Hispanics have been vocal and clear about their own needs, but there has been relatively little evidence that they saw themselves as members of a single reform process. This fragmentation has affected the structure of the social welfare institution, because it has tended to respond separately to each group, developing separate programs and separate structures as different needs have been identified. There has been little attention to planning for the whole. This fragmentation has been seized upon by critics as evidence of social welfare's inherent inefficiency and ineffectiveness.

We have noted some of the setbacks that the social welfare institution has suffered in the past few decades, but this period has also made important contributions. The growing self-awareness and assertiveness of women, blacks, Hispanics, the disabled, the elderly, the young, Vietnam veterans, and others have helped to keep temporizing values alive in the public consciousness during a period of general contraction and retrenchment in social welfare. These groups have heightened public recognition of a whole range of significant social problems, thus helping to set the stage for the next movement of the policy pendulum. Without the energy of these individual groups, it is possible that the dismantling of social welfare structures would have been even more profound, the retrenchment even deeper, and the damange to the institution even more severe.

Yet, these individual groups, each working in isolation, have created a multitude of separate constituencies, inadvertently fostering the idea that each social problem is the sole concern of one discrete and separate interest, not a shared concern of the whole community. This division has dissipated the potential energy that could be exerted on the political process and has underscored the feeling of many that only one element of the social welfare institution—the one that serves them alone—is of concern to them. This particularistic view is especially shortsighted when one considers that together these groups represent a majority of the American population. A process in which those outside the social welfare institution begin to develop cohesion and coherence would help the pendulum to gain momentum. To the extent that outside groups can agree on more holistic concepts of need and program, the social welfare institution can be energized into significant change and development.

A coming together of such groups will add potency and force to the outside process, maximizing the energy that has been generated by individual constituencies. In our discussion of soft services we used the concept of integrative needs as a way to look at potential commonalities in service provision. This has obvious relevance for the coalescence of the outside process. There are differences in the needs of each group, but there are also unexplored areas of common interest.

For example, if women are paid on the average fifty-nine cents for every dollar earned by men, that is a woman's issue. But it is also an issue of income maintenance, and if it can be seen in this integrative light, strategies can be developed that will help merge the energy of the women's movement with that of youths facing chronic unemployment or blacks who are underemployed. The financial and psychological deprivation in these cases may be very similar, and more can be achieved in coalition.

The same integrative approach might apply to the problem of family violence. Those concerned about child abuse or rape or protecting the elderly or battered wives may find common ground under this general concept and join to pursue common solutions. Medical services may also be perceived as an integrative need, with the developmentally disabled, minorities, the elderly, and other groups, all needing affordable, accessible health care.

The recognition of integrative needs depends to a large extent on the perception and definition of social problems and the priorities each group brings to a potential coalition. This use of integrative needs is a first step toward building coalitions. Such a perception does not need to eclipse the individual identity of any group; it becomes a matter of balance. A coalition does not preclude vigorous individual effort. It implies a joining together when such action can serve in a positive way and the separate pursuit of individual objectives when that course seems more productive.

A more potent and energized outside process can have enormous impact on the social welfare institution. This has, as we have discussed in earlier chapters, been the case in the past. The settlement house workers and other reformers of the Progressive Era, the labor organizers of the 1930s, the civil rights activists of the 1960s—all played an important role in preparing the way for the social welfare legislation that followed. It can be argued that their efforts helped to provide the energy by which the pendulum swung toward a more active period for social welfare. All of these movements contributed to the public recognition of certain severe social problems. Whether these were conditions of industrial safety during the Progressive Era, poverty and unemployment in the 1930s, or racial discrimination in the 1960s, members of the outside process made a vigorous appeal to the conscience of the country. Only then could action follow.

The outside process also helped to develop and popularize particular approaches and solutions to problems, from child labor laws at the turn of the century to the progressive income tax proposals of the Bull Moose Party of 1912, to collective bargaining and national unemployment insurance in the 1930s, to job training and voting rights in the 1960s.

The successful communication of the severity of social problems and the popularization of certain solutions depend heavily on the coherence and cohesion of the outside process. Obviously, if social norms are too severely flouted or if the message and the messengers seem divided and contradictory, the effects will be less successful and may even incur a backlash. The more cohesive and unitary the concept and the message, the more impact they are likely to have on the general public, and the more potential there is for achieving the kinds of changes which can help alleviate need.

We would argue, then, that a more unified and holistic *outside* process can help provide the energy to bring about change *inside* the social welfare institution, along the lines we described earlier in this chapter. The impetus for change cannot come solely from inside. The holistic vision that we argued is lacking throughout social welfare probably cannot be self-generated by the institution alone because of the very fragmentation and balkanization that create the need for reform. It is clear that what is needed is an interaction between outside and inside to bring about the climate for change.

New approaches must be found that can bring the two processes together. For the outside to organize, come together, and advocate in the most effective way—and for the inside to respond—is, in theory, one of the bases of political democracy. But such processes need structure, a structure that of late has not existed on the outside or the inside.

For the outside, the vehicle is the recognition of integrative needs and organized coalitions that work coherently and cohesively to influence the inside process. The inside requires similarly holistic approaches, since coalitions are essential on the inside as well as the outside if productive change is to be achieved. It is the political process that brings the inside and the outside together, exchanging ideas and helping to influence the general public as well. This in theory is the place at which the outside chooses those who will work for it on the inside and carry out its general mandate. In recent years the inside process has been significantly weakened, and the idea of social welfare as a holistic concept or even as a solution to shared needs has found few supporters within the policy-making process. This has been a period of retrenchment for social welfare and of distrust for government in general, brought about—as we have indicated—by numerous factors, many of them external to the social welfare institution. But it does seem clear that new directions for social welfare can only be brought about if they are forthrightly represented in the national political process.

REASSERTING SOCIAL WELFARE

Throughout this book we have argued that the current social welfare institution is characterized by imbalances that have a dysfunctional effect on the outcome of its programs and upon the support it receives. By examining such basic elements as values, technology, and structure, we have concluded that the social welfare institution is suffering from a high degree of balkanization and fragmentation of purpose, a condition that adversely affects it from the top levels, where funds are distributed, to the community level, where services are delivered and the recipients come into direct contact with the institution. It can be argued that the social welfare institution is experiencing the same kind of dissolution that other institutions in American society are facing.

To redress these imbalances, we have advocated a refocusing of thought and action toward more holistic approaches, both in what we have termed the outside process (those individuals and groups in need of or concerned with the institution's benefits) and the inside process (those charged with the actual conception and implementation of policy and program). Obviously, this perspective requires extensive further examination and refinement. We have confined ourselves in this analysis to the suggestion of the direction in which we feel movement is indicated. What does appear vital for those concerned with the strength and survival of social welfare is to begin to evolve new ways by which the institution can structure itself so as to realize its humanitarian intent in a context that is consistent with a system of pluralistic democracy.

As we noted in the Preface to this book, the American people have increasingly come to question the authority of public institutions and even their basic worth and place in society. This distrust has adversely affected the perception and strength of social welfare as one such institution. The question of the role of a public institution—what should it achieve—has therefore been raised in a very fundamental way. We would contend that a public institution such as social welfare has one primary mission: to mitigate the dehumanization and isolation of modern society, to augment individuals' feelings of self-worth and the compassion we hold for one another. History is replete with examples of great barbarity and great compassion; a public institution, to serve its social function, needs to be judged by the extent to which it achieves, encourages, and facilitates the more compassionate and humane side of our nature.

Index

Aaron, H., 119
Accountability, 105–110
  evaluation and, 105–107
  fiscal, 108–110
  skepticism and, 107–108
Addams, J., 5–6, 25, 115
The Affluent Society, 11
Aid to Dependent Children (ADC), 94
Aid for Families of Dependent Children (AFDC), 92, 94

Balkanization, 76–77
Barth, M. C., 120
Benedict, R., on civilization, 136
Benefits, error rates in distributing, 109
Beveridge Report, 107, 144
Blumer, M., on evolution of social problems, 98
Brodkin, E., 109
Brown v. Board of Education, 28
Buber, M., on social relationships, 136–137
Budget Reconciliation Act, 82
Burnout, 122
Burns, J. M., on government involvement in social policy change, 13

Caputo, D. A., 84
Carnegie, A., on philanthropy, 53
Carvalho, B. F., 51
Casework, psychiatry and, 43–44
Caseworkers
  problems of, 128
  roles of, 127–128
CCC. *See* Civilian Conservation Corps
Centralization, 49–51
  Great Society, 60–65
  New Deal, 57–60

CETA. *See* Comprehensive Employment and Training Act
Charitable organizations, national, 53
Charity Organization Society, 4–5
Cherniss, C., on staff discouragement, 122–123
Children's Bureau, 5
Civil rights, 28
  organizations, 9
Civil Rights Commission, 82
Civil Works Administration, 58–59
Civilian Conservation Corps, 58
Civilization, defined, 136
Client categorization, 116–118
Client displacement, 115–116
Cleveland, G., 54
Community Action Program, 62, 63
Comprehensive Employment and Training Act, 81, 93
Comprehensive Health Planning agencies, 84
Coolidge, C., social welfare policy under, 7
Council of Economic Advisers, 158
Council of Social Advisers, proposal for, 158
CWA. *See* Civil Works Administration

Darwinism, social, 22
Davis, K., and W. E. Moore, "Some Principles of Stratification," 36–38
Decentralization, 51–52
  Great Society, 60–65
  pre-Progressive Era, 52–54
  Progressive Era, 54–57
Delinquency, 9
de Tocqueville, A., 12, 53